# The Macular Degeneration Handbook

## Simple Solutions For Saving Your Sight

By Chet Cunningham

Agora Health Books
Baltimore, Maryland

Chet Cunningham
The Macular Degeneration Handbook: Simple Solutions For Saving Your Sight

**Published by Agora Health Books**

Alice Wessendorf, Managing Editor

Copyright 2007 by Agora Health Books
Copyright 1999/2001, 2003 by United Research Publishers

Library of Congress Control Number 98-61570

Previously published under the title
"The Macular Degeneration Handbook: Natural Ways to Prevent and Reverse It"

ISBN-10: 1-891434-37-3
ISBN-13: 978-1-891434-37-2
Printed and bound in the United States of America

Cover and book design by Gerrit Wessendorf

Agora Health Books
819 North Charles Street
Baltimore, Maryland 21201
www.AgoraHealthBooks.com

# The Macular Degeneration Handbook
## Simple Solutions For Saving Your Sight

By Chet Cunningham

Agora Health Books
Baltimore, Maryland

# DISCLAIMER

All material in this publication is provided for information only and may not be construed as medical advice or instruction. No action should be taken based solely on the contents of this publication; instead, readers should consult appropriate health professionals on any matter relating to their health and well-being.

The information and opinions provided in this book are believed to be accurate and sound, based on the best judgment available to the authors, but readers who fail to consult with appropriate health authorities assume the risk of any injuries. The publisher is not responsible for errors or omissions.

THE INFORMATION PRESENTED HERE HAS NOT BEEN EVALUATED BY THE U.S. FOOD AND DRUG ADMINISTRATION. THIS PRODUCT IS NOT INTENDED TO DIAGNOSE, TREAT, CURE, OR PREVENT ANY DISEASE.

# TABLE OF CONTENTS

# INTRODUCTION

For most of us the worst possible disaster that could happen to us would be to go...BLIND!

Just the thought of blindness is enough to make grown men tremble and shake. The idea of never being able to see again, not to see another sunset, not to see the look on our loved one's face, not to read a newspaper or magazine or watch a TV show or a movie gives us bad dreams.

Vision loss is a first cousin to blindness. In fact, it may be a step along a short or long road to your not being able to see.

Most of us who are over 40 know the growing problem of our arms not being long enough, so our eyes can focus on the printed page. This one is simple to fix with reading glasses. The other problem, seeing at a distance, is relatively easily fixed as well.

When your eyes start to degenerate and develop problems that can't be fixed with lenses and could lead to your losing 60 to 70 percent of your vision, then you dig in your claws, flex your muscles, and demand that something be done to fix the problem.

One of those serious eye diseases is called Age-related Macular Degeneration (AMD). There is no cure; we don't know for sure what causes it. It's case of a vital part of the retina becoming clogged with material that cuts down on our central vision, that part that lets us read the fine print.

Most of us have never heard of macular degeneration. Usually the first time a person hears the words they are out of the mouth of an optometrist or an ophthalmologist when he or she tells us that's what we have.

Panic? Weeping and wailing? Stiff upper lip? Depression? I'm sure that the doctors have seen all these reactions and many more. The most important reaction, though, is how you look at the situation when you get this diagnosis.

When macular degeneration is caught early there may be ways to slow, stop, or even reverse it. Most medical doctors don't subscribe to this idea, but it has a large and growing following.

Look at it this way. If there is no known medical cure or treatment, what can you lose trying to take better care of your eyes, in general, with the hope that such care will improve or slow or stop your macular degeneration?

As you will see in the following pages, one way to attack macular degeneration is to try to prevent any further degeneration and if possible, to reverse the problem.

There is growing evidence that the use of vitamins, minerals, and herbal remedies can do a lot to help anyone with macular degeneration.

They are not a cure-all or a panacea, but if the medical doctors can do nothing, what can you risk by trying these remedies?

My ophthalmologist told me that, yes, I had macular degeneration, as my optometrist had suggested. I had about a 20 percent loss of sight in my right eye. I should check my vision daily on a wall chart. If there was any abrupt change in my right eye vision, I should contact him immediately. Otherwise, set up a six-month return appointment, and he would evaluate it then.

He told me to do nothing for six months. Was I supposed to sit there and let my eye lose another 20 percent and then go back to see him? Not a chance. This is my eyesight we're talking about here.

I want to do everything that has even a remote chance of stopping the deterioration and, if possible, reversing the problem with the buildup on my macula. Research. I was determined to find out everything anyone had ever said about stopping macular degeneration and perhaps reversing it. You have the result in your hands.

Yes, it's going to take some work on your part. You're going to have to change some eating habits, dig into vitamins and minerals and herbal products with a zest, get enough exercise, drink enough water, and after all of this, there is a good possibility that you can stop and even reverse the macular degeneration now affecting your eyes.

The alternative? The medics can do a risky laser eye surgery, killing off cells with the hope to stop the wet type of macular degeneration. Sometimes it works, but it also kills off more good cells. This is risky and done only as a last resort.

So, this is the situation:

❶ You're in a no-win situation with your doctor.

❷ By following a few simple life-rules and eating and additive programs, you stand a good chance of stopping the macular degeneration and perhaps reversing it.

❸ If you do nothing, you could lose nearly total vision in the affected eye, or in both eyes.

❹ You could go blind.

Not much of a problem making this decision, is there?

So, let's charge on and see just what you need to do to help Mother Nature stop and perhaps reverse your macular degeneration.

# 1 What is Macular Degeneration?

With macular degeneration, your macula is clogged with material that clouds and blocks the portion of the eye that gives you sharp, central vision and color definition.

Usually it happens to both eyes, but not always. The condition can sneak up on you gradually, especially if it's only in one eye. The onset can also be sudden, and you'll know something is wrong at once. This condition is never the result of over—or misusing your eyes. It's not a disease, and we know of no cause—neither do we have a cure for it.

If both eyes are affected, you may not be able to drive or read, and you may have dark blotches on your vision.

Since this problem deals only with the central part of the macula, you still have side vision. Macular degeneration rarely leaves a person totally blind.

## Can you tell if you have this problem?

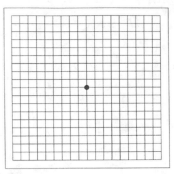

Yes. Look at graph paper. Stare at the very center of a sheet of graph paper.

Do some of the lines above and below tend to waver or bow upward or downward or go in and out on the sides? If so, then you have an early stage of macular degeneration.

If you see a blank or dark spot in the center of a picture or a page in your field of vision, you may also have macular degeneration.

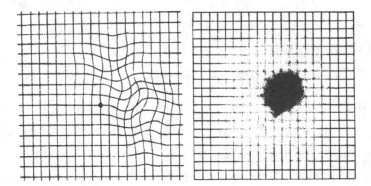

You should see an ophthalmologist at once. He or she will be able to confirm your suspicions, tell you what type of macular degeneration you have, wet or dry, and tell you if there is anything that can be done to treat it.

## Just how does this degeneration happen?

To see this let's look at a picture of the eye. This is a cross section showing the cornea, the lens, the pupil, and how light comes through the pupil and is focused on the back of the eye on the retina.

The retina is the "receiver." It picks up the light images, translates them into electrical energy, and sends them via the optic nerves to the brain, and, magically, you see.

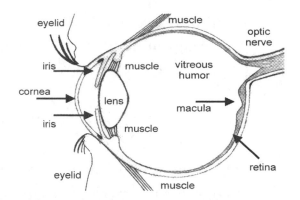

The light focuses on the center of the retina, described by some as a bull's-eye. This is where your sharp vision happens, where you can see intricate patterns and read the fine print.

The rest of your retina is also picking up light images. These are what you see "out of the corner of your eye."

These peripheral vision images are not affected by macular degeneration, no matter how serious the malady becomes. For this reason there will always be partial vision around the sides of your eyes and the sides of your vision pattern.

The macula itself is a thin and highly fragile material at the center of your retina. It has several layers. In the outer one are light-sensing cells that enable you to have your sharp vision.

Under that layer of light-sensing cones, there are two more layers that nourish the light cells and at the same time digest and remove the waste from the cells. The digesting layer is called the epithelium, and it disposes of the discarded cone tips.

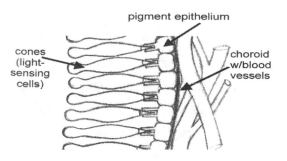

The next layer is called the choroid and it contains blood vessels. This part brings in nourishment in the blood and also takes out the waste from the digested cell tips.

## The dry type of Macular Degeneration

How does this system break down and cause trouble?

For some reason the tips of the cones do not get digested properly by the pigment epithelium. Since they aren't digested correctly, they can't be passed on to the choroid and transferred out of the system.

This buildup of the undigested cone tips makes small areas of the pigment epithelium swell up and soon die. Soon the undigested material turns yellow and begins to collect under the pigment epithelium.

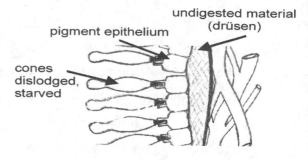

Since parts of the macula are dying, due to the buildup and the undigested material, it leaves small "holes" in the image the retina is receiving. No signal would be sent through a part where the macula is not functioning. This can create the appearance of wavy lines in your vision. This might show up on a door or window casing, on a tall building, or simply on the traffic lanes painted on the roadway.

It also can cause blurry letters on signs and when reading, since part of the signal showing that letter does not get through the dead area of the macula. This type of macular degeneration is called "dry." Dry macular degeneration is usually the gradual kind that develops over a period of time. It is the less severe of the two types.

Why does this deterioration take place?

No one knows for sure. One theory is that after years of poor diet and perhaps lifestyle choices, the choroid that feeds the cones becomes clogged with cholesterol and perhaps calcium deposits, rendering them no longer able to feed the cones.

When this happens they evidently can't properly digest the cone tips that must be digested. Also, oxygen is prevented from reaching this area of the retina and that starves the cells, and they begin to die.

Some experts believe that oxidation is an important factor. It may be part of the problem in blood vessel diseases, which could then result in clogged capillaries that feed the cones and result in their death.

Perhaps the lack of antioxidants in the person's diet allows the free radicals to have free rein, resulting in more blocked capillaries.

If for any reason the blood flow to the retina is slowed or reduced, then normal antioxidants in that blood can't prevent the natural oxidation damage of the retina, which only speeds up the damage to the macula.

Another factor in macular degeneration is the development of aging spots called drusen. These spots on the pigment epithelium occur in about 30 percent of adults, and in many cases there is no problem with their vision. It is not known entirely how these spots develop, but it is thought that they are the result of insufficient flushing of the digested wastes into the bloodstream.

## The wet type of Macular Degeneration

The wet type may result in a rapid and severe loss of sight in one or both eyes. This often happens when for unknown reasons abnormal new blood vessels grow under the pigment epithelium and leak fluid or blood.

When this fluid builds up it causes the macula to bulge, which distorts your vision, often resulting in a dark spot in the center of your vision. This also can mean that straight lines look wavy and can wiggle all over the place. Check this on your Amsler grid.

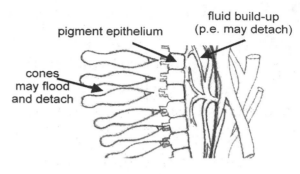

## What is an Amsler grid?

This is a square sheet of paper with one-eighth-inch squares with a black dot in the center.

You focus on the black dot and watch to see if the lines remain straight or start to bow and bend and waver. If they do, you have some stage of macular degeneration. It's a simple test and one that you should do every day at home if you have AMD. If there is any sudden change, you should contact your ophthalmologist at once.

In the wet type, the pigment epithelium may become detached from the cones. The cones may also be flooded with fluid or blood and this can cause them to separate from their "stalls" on the pigment epithelium which will quickly cause them to die and leave another black spot in your central vision.

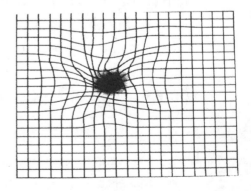

## Available medical treatments

First, let's talk about dry macular degeneration. About 90 percent of all people with AMD, have the dry type. This is the least severe and causes the least vision loss.

Unfortunately, there is also no medical procedure to reverse dry macular degeneration. As we said before there is no proven cause of macular degeneration. So, we call it a condition. Your doctor will probably tell you this, and then say go home and use the Amsler test chart every day to watch for any significant change in your vision. If you find any, give him a call at once.

Then he or she will tell you to always wear a good pair of sunglasses and a hat with a bill on it to protect your eyes when out in the sun, and to come back and see him in six months. That's all?

That's about it. There simply is nothing at this time that medical science can do to help reverse or cure dry macular degeneration. There may be some help in the future but for right now there is nothing.

We'll talk about some ways many forward-looking ophthalmologists think you may be able to slow, stop, and even reverse your AMD. These include the proper diet, vitamins, minerals and some herbal remedies, and healthy exercise. But we'll get to that later.

For the wet type of macular degeneration, there are some medical procedures. The wet type is the more serious and often results in nearly the total loss of the central vision in the eye or eyes it attacks.

## Laser surgery

For those with the wet type of AMD there is laser surgery. This procedure uses a small laser beam to stop the growth of the sight-threatening new blood vessels that are growing over the retina and cutting off vision. Your doctor will tell you this is a last resort to try to help your vision.

What the laser beam does is cauterize or seal up the small leaks in the blood vessels in the retina. While it can't restore lost vision, it is a temporary stopgap to prevent the spread of the leakage. Some of the laser beams are bound to destroy some of the good tissue and vessels, which may cut down on your vision a little bit more.

This is a temporary procedure. After a few months the laser may be needed again to seal off new leaks and again some more of the healthy cells will be destroyed.

Remember that this laser use is for those with the more serious wet type of AMD.

If new blood vessels begin to grow under the pigment epithelium, the laser can't be used and the other choices are drugs, radiation, or surgery.

Few of the 10 percent of those with wet type AMD will be good patients for laser surgery. Most of the others should try the nutritional and vitamin-minerals-herbals that will be suggested later in the book.

Most doctors will recommend that only the patients with the most severe cases of wet macular degeneration should even think about laser surgery. Patients should try the alternative medicine we'll talk about soon.

## Radiation treatments

Ionizing radiation treatment can also be used for the most serious wet AMD cases. This is the same treatment as used for cancer and other diseases.

With any radiation use within the body, the goal is to kill unwanted cells. But in almost every instance, to get the bad ones, many of the good cells are killed as well. In some cases this is not important, but in a limited area such as the center of the retina, it can be vital. Destroying the cells can help delay the growth of new blood cells over the retina, and this is the good part.

As with the laser, this treatment must be repeated, with more and more of the limited number of cells destroyed.

Radiation is a last-hope effort for the seriously impaired wet AMD patient.

## Drugs in the anti-angiogenesis class

These drugs are just starting to be used in extreme cases of wet macular degeneration. The long word means this: "Anti" is against; "Angio" is a Greek word meaning blood vessel; "Genesis" is another Greek word that means to be born or to come into being.

Doctors use one of these drugs to stop any new growth of blood vessels in the wet form of macular degeneration. You've heard of two of these drugs. One is the infamous thalidomide, a drug that caused serious birth defects when it was mistakenly given to pregnant women in the 1960s. It is now used against the wet form of AMD and so far it has been safe with no side effects. It is a highly expensive drug, and it has no proven track record of success yet.

Another drug in this same class and used for the same purpose is the recently developed drug interferon. There is much speculation here and no firm pattern of success. Some of those researching and experimenting with the drug think it may have more value when used in conjunction with laser surgery. Interferon does have serious side effects including fever and headaches that resemble the flu, muscle aches, and chills. Over half of those who used interferon reported these side effects.

## Retinal cell transplants

In the next 10 to 12 years there may be a procedure to repair macular degeneration damage. It's simply transplanting healthy retinal cells where those have died. Right now it is still in the experimental and research stage, but if it works, it could be the one hope for many with serious retinal problems.

## Aspirin and ibuprofen are no no's

If your doctor suggests that the use of one or two aspirin a day could help your AMD by thinning your blood and improving blood flow to the retinas, ask him a lot of questions. While increased blood flow to the retina can help curb and slow macular degeneration, there are other ways to do it without the risk of the NSAIDs.

Risk? Some researchers say that the NSAIDs can actually be a cause of macular degeneration when they cause retinal hemorrhages in the retina blood vessels. These tiny leaks develop into wet AMD. Ibuprofen is said to cause retinal hemorrhages in eyes not yet harmed by AMD. People who already have AMD have extremely delicate eye vessels, and many of the same patients also have high blood pressure. This double jolt can be tremendously damaging to the delicate blood vessels in the eyes.

So, most ophthalmologists will not suggest the aspirin route. There are other ways to improve blood flow to your eyes with no risk whatsoever. These include better nutrition and special nutrients with anti-inflammatory action such as omega-3, garlic, vitamin E, omega-6, fatty acids, and magnesium. We'll deal more with this later.

# Photodynamic therapy

One final medical type treatment in the experimental stages is called photodynamic therapy. In this treatment, surgeons cause the production of free radicals in the retina by using special molecules that make cells more sensitive to light. They do this in the diseased part of the retina, letting the body's natural oxidation process destroy the unwanted blood vessel growth. This again is an extreme procedure still in the experimental stage, and if or when it comes into the mainstream of eye surgery, it will be for the most advanced cases of macular degeneration.

# 2 Your Best Alternative

Let's say you have dry macular degeneration. What can you do? There's no medical procedure to help you. The doctor says yeah, you've got it, do this eye test every day and come back and see me in six months.

So you sit there and let your eyes get worse for six months and go back and he says, "Yep, it's spreading, but there's nothing I can do to help you." That's no medical solution.

This could be one way.

More and more doctors around the country are recognizing that vitamins, minerals, nutrition, and herbal supplements just might be able to slow down, even stop, and reverse dry macular degeneration. If you are one of those people who think that vitamins and additives and herbal remedies are a bunch of hokum, look at it this way. You have no other path to take.

These vitamins and additives, right now, are one possible way that you just might be able to slow down and stop the macular degeneration now taking place in your eyes. There is no other option, medical or otherwise.

If this doesn't work, then how fast the course of your condition worsens is up to you. My vote is to take a shot at the vitamin-supplement treatment. One good fact: It can't hurt you, and it could be a sight saver.

As with any regimen you set up for your body's health, it's always a good idea to check with your ophthalmologist before moving ahead. Take a list of vitamins and minerals you think you should be taking to help slow or reduce your macular degeneration.

If your doctor blows you off, saying this is all a bunch of unfounded foolishness, perhaps you should find a different doctor who has some idea of the research and development being done on the part vitamins and minerals play in the health of the eye.

What your doctor should tell you is which of the vitamins or minerals or supplements might be bad for you to take, taking into consideration the state of your health and your general condition. This way you might be able to prevent an overdose or a conflict between some of the items.

Some good news at last. Let's start with:

## Vitamins

Back to the basics. Good old vitamin C is the first stop on your vitamin diet. It is pretty well established that for the dry type of AMD, vitamin C will help prevent blood vessels in the retina from breaking and prevent the growth of new blood vessels on the macula. No laboratory, double-blind proof, but the case studies that individual doctors have made support the idea that vitamin C can help.

Now, along with the vitamin C, there are substances called bioflavonoids. These are usually present in nature with vitamin C. For example your rich-in-vitamin C fruits, such as berries, lemons, grapes, plums, grapefruit, apricots, and cherries are all also high in bioflavonoids. This material helps the body to utilize the vitamin C, and while not essential, it makes the vitamin C you take just that much more effective.

One common source of bioflavonoids is rose hips. Other sources of bioflavonoids include supplements such as quercetin, extract of bilberry, ginkgo biloba, cranberry, or grapeseed. Of these bilberry is the one specifically targeted for the eyes; it is said to be a big help in night vision.

Your minimum daily dosage of vitamin C should be from 2,000 to 10,000 mg. On the bioflavonoids go from 200 to 400 mg.

## Cold water fish and fish oils

One of the best sources of vitamin A and D is fish. The cold water type: trout, tuna, salmon, mackerel, cod, and even sardines.

These fish furnish vitamin A that is easy to absorb and utilize. It even outscores beta-carotene in this aspect. The liver will pick up and store any excess vitamin A, and it can be drawn upon when the eye needs it.

Also from these fish you'll get omega-3 fatty acids. The jury reports this fatty acid is good for you. One of the results of the omega-3 is a decrease in blood clotting. This means your blood vessels in the retina will stay clear and discourage macular degeneration from gaining any ground.

It's best to simply eat fish or seafood three times a week, but some people don't like fish. Now that they have AMD, they need to learn to eat it. The other option is with a supplement of the oil. Be sure the supplement isn't rancid. If it is, it can do you more harm than good. To test capsules, break one open and smell it. If it's rancid, you'll know it. Take them back for a refund.

## Beta-carotene with vitamin A

Beta-carotene is a vital element to add to your diet. Here, the more the better. It can be harmful only if you don't get enough vitamin E, which we'll cover later. As a safeguard also take vitamin A to help your body convert the beta-carotene into useful elements. The minimum daily intake should be from 15,000 to 25,000 IU. If you are pregnant, keep it to 15,000 IU.

## Magnesium

This mineral is important to many parts and functions of your body. We're mainly interested in magnesium because it helps provide a good blood flow to the eyes, maintains the proper fluid balance in the cells, and, at the same time, reduces muscle spasms. Magnesium also plays a vital role in the metabolism and absorption of calcium in your body. It is important to the correct functioning of your heart and in literally 100 other bio-chemical actions that take place in the body every day.

Magnesium supplements should be from 300 to 500 mg, usually taken at bedtime.

## Vitamin E

You may already be taking vitamin E. It does a lot of different things for the body, but is essential to the health of your eyes. It helps keep oxidation away from your eyes and helps to maintain healthy blood vessels in them as well. Then they won't start leaking. One form of vitamin E, called alpha tocopherol, is layered across the retina. The thin part is where macular degeneration begins. Your daily dose of 800 IU will help prevent this. Most vitamin E doses are listed at 400, so you'll want to double that.

## Garlic

Many people love it for the taste. Now you should love it for the good it can do for your eyes. Garlic will help keep your blood from clotting, help raise your HDL cholesterol, and lower the LDL. The best way to get it is fresh in the foods you eat. If not that way the second method is in the garlic pills on the market. Garlic is high in sulfur content, which can help the production of glutathione in your body.

How much garlic? Fresh, maybe a clove a day. In pill form 1,000 mg. Enjoy. Oh, there are always breath mints.

## Zeaxanthin and Lutein

Here are a couple of tongue twisters that can really help your eyes. These are two yellow carotenoid pigments in your eyes that are sun filters cutting out blue light from your central retina. They are vital. When these are depleted or in short supply, the retina can suffer and macular degeneration can begin or increase.

Both of these compounds are found in spinach, collard greens, turnip greens, mustard greens, and kale. People who eat a good supply of these greens tend to have fewer cases of AMD—a 43 percent reduction in risk than those who don't, according to a report in the *Journal of the American Medical Association.*

Smokers, people with light blue eyes, and menopausal women have half as much natural lutein and zeaxanthin in the back of their eyes as the rest of us, so they are more susceptible to AMD. However, a big helping of spinach could be wasted if you are also having a meal with high beta-carotene food or supplements. The two tend to fight in the body to see who will be absorbed. In a case like this, one or the other gets wasted. So you may need to alternate meals.

You should also eat foods that are relatively high in lutein and zeaxanthin. The following table gives combined values for some fruits and vegetables.

| Food (100 grams) | Lutein and Zeaxanthin mcg | Food (100 grams) | Lutein and Zeaxanthin mcg |
|---|---|---|---|
| Grapefruit, pink, raw | 3.362 | Pepper, red | 6.800 |
| Green beans | 0.740 | Pepper, yellow, raw | 0.770 |
| Greens, collard | 16.300 | Plum, raw | 0.240 |
| Kale | 21.900 | Prune, dried | 0.120 |
| Kiwi fruit, raw | 0.180 | Pumpkin | 1.500 |
| Leek, raw | 1.900 | Spinach, cooked, drained | 12.600 |
| Lettuce, iceberg | 1.400 | Spinach, raw | 10.200 |
| Lettuce, leaf | 1.800 | Squash, summer | 1.200 |
| Lettuce, romaine | 5.700 | Swiss chard, raw | 11.000 |
| Okra, raw | 6.800 | Tangerine | 0.020 |
| Peach, dried | 0.188 | Tomato juice, canned | 0.330 |
| Peas, green | 1.700 | Tomato paste, canned | 0.190 |
| Pepper, green, raw | 0.700 | Tomato, raw | 0.100 |

## Selenium

This one helps protect cell membranes, including those in your retina, from oxidation. It also has antiviral properties. Selenium is one part of glutathione peroxidase. A supplement here of about 200 mcg is sufficient.

## Taurine

Here we have one of the amino acids that is important to keeping your eyes in good shape and your blood up to par. Daily dose of the supplement should be 1,000 mg, and taken between, not during, your meals.

## N-acetyl cysteine (NAC)

This supplement has only one function, to keep your glutathione levels up high where they should be. Take 500 mg two or three times a day.

## Zinc

Zinc aids in releasing vitamin A from your liver. If you take a good multivitamin daily, you probably are getting enough zinc. Check your bottle. You need 15 to 30 mg a day.

## Hydrochloric Acid

A supplement of hydrochloric acid can help if you don't have enough natural stomach acid. A pill of 250 mg of beta hydrochloric acid should be enough. Remember to take it with a meal.

## Coenzyme Q-10

This is an antioxidant with a lot of punch that will give your heart a boost and increase circulation at the same time. All right, that's quite a shopping list. But each of these vitamins or minerals could be the one that will stop or slow your macular degeneration.

Look over the list again. Some of them may be covered in that good complete multiple vitamin-mineral daily pill you're taking already. If so, you can eliminate that one from your shopping list.

Look around. Some of these basic vitamins and herbs are now available at wholesale stores such as Costco, or others like this. They often are membership stores that provide bulk shopping with good savings.

You might want to be selective and add certain items on a monthly or weekly basis. It's no fun suddenly to have to take 40 pills every night and morning. But remember, these are supplements and vitamins that many doctors say will be a help with your macular degeneration.

## Picking a good multivitamin

We've talked about taking supplements and additives in addition to your multivitamin pills. What should a good one contain? How do you know a good one when it hits you right in the pocketbook?

Here are some standards to shoot for. Not all of these vitamins and minerals will be in every multivitamin you check. Get the one that covers as many bases as possible, then fill in with additional items that you need.

Here is an alphabetical list of some standards to go by to judge your multivitamin mineral capsules against.

### A Vitamins: 5,000 to 10,000 IU

Most brands of multivitamins today don't contain any vitamin A. Vitamin A is important for anyone with eye problems. Beta-carotene is converted in the body to vitamin A, but this change is not always complete. For this reason many experts suggest you take additional vitamin A to be sure that the conversion is complete to supply the eyes with the needed vitamin A. It comes in liquid and pill form.

## B Vitamins

There are a number of the B vitamins: All are essential to the good functioning of your body. We're mainly concerned with your eyes, and they will suffer if you are deficient in any of the B vitamins. Daily doses of these include:

| | |
|---|---|
| B-1 | 25-50 mg |
| B-2 | 25-100 mg |
| B-3 | 50-100 mg |
| B-5 | 50-100 mg |
| B-6 | 50-100 mg |
| B-12 | 100-200 mg |
| Biotin | 100-300 mg |
| Choline | 50-100 mg |
| Folic Acid | 200-800 mg |
| Inositol | 150-300 mg |

As a footnote, the brand of multivitamins I'm checking right now does not show any B-3, B-5, or choline. You might want to check the brand that you're taking.

## Beta-carotene: 10,000 IU

Vital to good eyesight. About half of the beta-carotene ingested is converted to vitamin A. This is turned into pigments that aid in night vision. Be sure to take vitamin E when taking beta-carotene, since the two work together.

### Boron: 1-5 mg

Basically a chemical element that helps maintain strong bones.

### Calcium: Men: 500 mg, Women: 1,200 mg

Calcium is a major component for good health of the whole body. Most calcium is in the bones and teeth, but it also plays a part in many other functions.

### Chromium: 200 mcg

Helps your body maintain a normal function by balancing your sugar and insulin. It's a trace mineral which helps synthesize fatty acids and cholesterol. Many people have too little in their systems.

### Copper: 1-5 mg

Helps build blood components that move oxygen to your cells. Helps with protein metabolism.

### C Vitamins: 2,000 mg (when healthy);10,000 mg (when ill)

A strong antioxidant that joins the others to fight free radicals and stop oxidation of cholesterol particles. Strengthens blood vessels. Helps your immune system function. High vitamin C diet helps you live longer, healthier.

### D Vitamins: 400 IU

Most multivitamins have this one at this potency. Check yours. D is important to the body generally, but don't overdo it. You pick up vitamin D when your skin is exposed to sunlight and through nutrition. Cod liver oil and salmon are two good natural sources.

## Magnesium: 300 mg

This is a much higher daily dose than most multivitamins contain. Magnesium is tremendously important to bodily function involving bones, soft tissue, and fluids. It is important for regular heart and lung function and for energy production. It's vital to your body in hundreds of ways. Many multivitamins have less than 10 mg. You may need a supplement here.

## Manganese: 10 mg

Manganese is one of those trace minerals you don't need much of for good health; but the part you need you really need, or it can cause all sorts of problems. What it does is activate a lot of enzymes that put the B-vitamins to work. It gets in on the growth of your skeleton and formation of sex hormones. It also keeps your nervous system working. Most multivitamin minerals don't include manganese.

## Selenium: 25 mcg

Another trace mineral the body uses. This one is a potent antioxidant that works with vitamin E to prevent the polyunsaturated fats oxidation. In other words it's a good one. Again, not in most multivitamin pills.

## Zinc: 20 mg

Zinc is the most thoroughly researched of all the vitamin-minerals, and the experts say that it has a strong role in slowing and perhaps preventing macular degeneration. We know for sure that when there is a lack of zinc in the body, there is a deterioration of the macula. It has also been established that zinc helps vitamin A to be sent from the liver so it can be used in strengthening eye tissue. Interestingly, pumpkin seeds are one of the best sources of zinc.

## Supplements for the eyes

As more and more customers began asking for individual supplements for the good of their eyes, some firms began to experiment, making multiple vitamin and mineral once-a-day capsules that are put together to help those of us with eye problems.

It began slowly, but now a quick survey showed that there are 29 different multivitamin and mineral supplements now on the market aimed specifically at the eyes.

If your eye specialist suggested you try a regimen of vitamins, minerals, and supplements for the good of your eyes, try to get one that is composed of those special ingredients that you need.

You'll want to be sure to get one that has lots of antioxidants such as beta-carotene, vitamin C and E, selenium, Quercetin, bioflavonoids, bilberry, and ginkgo biloba. You'll want to see in them the amino acids like L-glutamine, L-glutathione, L-cysteine, and N-acetyl cysteine.

You probably won't find all of the components you need in any single one of the commercial products. Check them out with a list in hand and find as many of them as you can. Then you'll want to add to them with individual capsules of garlic or bilberry or whatever else you need.

Here is a list of some of the eye multivitamins and minerals with the best list of ingredients. Check them out: Bright Eyes, Cata-RX, Eye Formula, Eye Power, Ocuvite, Ocucare, OcuDyne, and Oxi-Freeda. One of these should come closer than the off-the-shelf standard multivitamin supplement.

# 3 Good Nutrition to Fight Macular Degeneration

If you have dry macular degeneration or the first stages of the wet type, your ophthalmologist probably will say he or she can't help you, all you can do is watch and wait.

Not true. You can start an aggressive attack with a vitamin and mineral program that we talked about in the last chapter. In addition, a study by the University of Wisconsin Medical School indicated "diets rich in saturated fat and cholesterol have been found to increase the risk of macular degeneration by 80 percent." So paying attention to nutrition seems to be a promising approach.

You can easily begin a program of "healthy-eye" eating to help your eyes. You don't like spinach? Tough, learn to love it—it may help you slow, stop, or even reverse your macular degeneration.

How do you do this? Here are some suggestions.

Supplements of vitamins and minerals are fine, but experts say that most of those same elements are much more potent and effective if they are received in the body through their natural sources...food. A diet that is especially helpful to your eyes is also beneficial to the rest of your body.

For example, foods high in vitamin C help your eyes, but vitamin C is essential to many other parts of your body as well. So don't think that a special "eye diet" is just for your eyes. Every one of the special minerals and vitamins and supplements will be working all over your body.

Before we get into specific foods, let's talk a few minutes about nutrition in general.

## The big fat flap

More has been written lately about fat in the diet than any other subject in years. "Low fat," "no fat," and "reduced fat" are labels that you see every day on food packages.

Low-fat diets have been the rage every six months or so, as more and more people try the best they can to eat better so they can stay in better health.

Quickly the problem of what kind of fat we're talking about comes to the front. There are three kinds of fat we use daily; one is the saturated fat type that remains a solid at room temperature. This includes butter, lard, and coconut oil.

Another kind is polyunsaturated fat. It is liquid at room temperature and includes cooking oils that are made from corn and safflower. The third kind of fat is mono-unsaturated oil that comes from olives, grapeseed, or avocados. Monounsaturated oil is stable and contains the essential oils you need for your body to function correctly.

For years the word has been that polyunsaturated fats are much better for your body than the hard saturated fats. This is not necessarily true.

Tests have shown that polyunsaturated fats can do just as much damage to your system as their solid cousins, the saturated fats. The big difference is how stable both fats are. The unsaturated ones are much less stable and tend to oxidize easily. This means they go rancid. When the oils oxidize in your body, they begin to oxidize everything they come in contact with. Your body has to fight off this oxidation with its antioxidant troops. Often there aren't enough of them. When the oxidation takes place in your eye, it can lead to serious trouble.

The stable, solid saturated fats do not become rancid so easily and present fewer problems for your body.

Of course, it is simple to see that if you go to extremes by eating too much of any fat, your body will be screaming at you to stop. The solution is to stay away from the polyunsaturated fats and eat those stable saturated ones, or better yet, the mono-unsaturated fats. Many of the margarines on the market now have all three kinds of fat in them. It is a good idea to remember to use these fats in moderation.

So, what about monounsaturated oils such as olive oil, canola oil, and avocado oil? Yes, they are better. They are stable so they won't go rancid so quickly and have the essential oils your body demands. Olive oil is usually considered the best of the three.

Have you ever heard of omega-3 oils?

Most of us haven't. That's a component of cold water fish such as cod, mackerel, and salmon. If you eat salmon twice a week you'll get an adequate supply of unsaturated essential omega-3 oil. Hey, salmon is good. Experts in the field say that this oil will help improve the "good" high-density (HDL) cholesterol, cut down on arterial disease, and decrease inflammation. Sounds good.

We haven't talked about trans-fatty oil. This is hydrogenated oil and is in margarine, potato chips, cookies, most baked goods, and processed foods. Avoid these hydrogenated oils as often as possible. Chop margarine out of your shopping list and use butter, but in smaller amounts. Check the new no-fat material that some manufacturers are now using for items such as potato chips. They call it Olean, and it is supposed to produce fat-free potato chips. Some people have reported that Olean gave them an upset stomach. The latest report is that it worked for some people and made others slightly ill.

That's the story on fats and oils.

## Carbohydrates good—carbohydrates bad

Every diet you've ever seen has a part about good old carbs, said to be great for the dieter. Sometimes they are right, sometimes wrong.

Carbohydrates are in most everything that we eat. They are listed on most packaging. You probably don't realize what a wide variety of foods have carbohydrates in them. Take a look on the supermarket shelves: bread, pasta, cereal, brown sugar, canned peas, raw honey, potato chips, even an apple, and a long loaf of French bread all have carbs.

Your body loves carbohydrates. They are the easiest of all foods to utilize since they break down into glucose, the easy-to-digest form of sugar. The body then burns up the glucose, turning it into energy, and we come out even. Of course if you take in more carbohydrates than you burn up, they turn into fat and linger around the body. Too much of a good carb is a bad thing.

Carbohydrates can be tricky. Actually there are two types of carbs. The first kind is called natural. That is the apples, the peas, the potatoes—all the foods that are harvested and eaten with little or no processing.

On the other hand, we have the foods that are highly processed. Sugar is refined: wheat is processed for bread, pasta, or cereal. During the milling, refining, and processing, many of the natural vitamins, minerals, fiber, and enzymes are pulled out. When you eat these foods, your body has to supply the missing nutrients it needs to digest the food so it can serve as body fuel.

So, the best carbohydrates are those in whole grains, vegetables, beans, and fruits.

Those natural carbohydrates are better for you. They don't require the body to supply any additives to help digest them.

As with all nutrition, work for a balance. Carbohydrates are good, but if you eat more of them than you burn off with exercise, you start to put on weight.

## Now for the big one: cholesterol

The big cholesterol flap continues. For 20 years doctors promoted an all-out assault on cholesterol, blaming it for half the ailments of mankind. They worked to bring down the total blood cholesterol with diet and drugs. They told us to go easy on red meat, eggs, and all things that come from a dairy cow.

Today doctors take a different tack. They say there are two types of cholesterol: HDL (high density lipoprotein) the good, and LDL (low density lipoprotein) the bad. LDL cholesterol can cause a buildup in the arteries, which restricts blood flow. HDL cholesterol removes excess lipids/fats from your blood.

So now we worry about a healthy ratio between the good and the bad cholesterol. The next hope is that the HDL will not be oxidized.

Anything that blocks your arteries, and keeps a normal flow of blood from the eyes, is going to hurt them. That's why we worry about cholesterol because it affects the eyes perhaps quicker than other parts of the body.

So, how can we raise the good HDL count? The traditional way for the rest of the body also will help with your eyes: plenty of reasonable exercise. Don't run a marathon every weekend, but do get a good workout that is in keeping with your age and body condition, three to five times a week. Seven times wouldn't hurt.

What's the best exercise for any age?

Walking. It takes no partner or opponent, you can do it anytime day or night, you don't need any equipment, you can even do it on a treadmill in your living room while you're watching your favorite TV show.

What else can help? Eat lots of garlic, eat more soy protein, and get in your two to three meals of fish a week. Some nutritionists say that a glass or two of wine four times a week will aid in building up your good HDL cholesterol. Researchers at Howard University were surprised to find that teetotalers were more than twice as likely to have AMD than those who regularly drink wine. Don't go overboard here. Your liver can suffer if you drink too much alcohol. You need that liver in top-notch shape to bring vitamin A and glutathione to your system. Both of these substances are vital for good eye health.

## Do your eyes need extra vitamins and supplements?

For years I was snobbish about vitamins, minerals, health foods, and supplements. Hey, I was eating a good diet. I was in good health. Why fool around with those extra vitamins? I'd heard that if you get too many of most of them they wind up being passed off in your urine anyway.

When macular degeneration blindsided me, and the doctors said there was no cure, no medical procedures to even stop it, let alone reverse it, I developed a new appreciation for anything that might help.

My research through many books and doctors has shown me that while the medics can do nothing to slow or stop AMD, there very well may be a dietary way to do the job. Nobody is saying that these crucial vitamins and minerals and homeopathic compounds absolutely and without fail will stop AMD.

But, it's the ONLY WAY now known that even has a ghost of a chance of stopping it. So I'm giving it a try. I'm on a six-month regimen to use most, if not all, of the supplements and vitamins and healthy foods that I can, with the hope that it will do some good to slow or stop my own macular degeneration.

Doctors across the country have used this treatment, and many say they can show on many patients where it has absolutely stopped macular degeneration, especially the dry type. That's what I have and what I'm fighting even as I write these words.

Most multivitamins also contain trace minerals needed by the body. The only trouble here is that most of the brands you can buy over the counter at grocery and drug stores, have a small percentage of even the minimum daily requirement and only a smaller fraction of the potency that the experts say is needed for fighting macular degeneration.

## How much is enough?

Nobody knows. Some specialists in eye surgery and care have put together a list of the most important vitamins, minerals, and supplements. They say you should have 2,000 mg of vitamin C. The US-prescribed minimum daily requirement (MDR) is listed at 60 mg.

The MDR for vitamin A shows as 5,000 IU. Most eye specialists ask me to take 25,000 IUs to help protect and maybe save my eyes.

Generally the suggestions for eye care are for more potency than the MDR. I'm going along with the eye experts. What else can any of us do? We play our cards, and we hope we have the winning hand.

If you have macular degeneration and want to give the massive vitamin-mineral-supplement route a try, here is a target list for you to use in the pharmacy, grocery store, or health food stores. The health food stores will have the best variety and types of vitamins and supplements to choose from.

Copy this chart, or take the book with you to the store, and check out their multivitamin offerings. This way you'll have to take fewer pills. Right now I'm on 11 pills in the morning and down to about six at night.

| | |
|---|---|
| ■ Vitamin A | 25,000 IU |
| ■ Bioflavonoids | 400 mg |
| ■ Bilberry | 160 mg |
| ■ Beta-carotene | 25,000 IU |
| ■ Vitamin C | 2,000 mg |
| ■ Coenzyme Q-10 | 200 mg |
| ■ Vitamin E | 800 mg |
| ■ Garlic | 1,000 mg |
| ■ Ginkgo biloba | 120 mg |
| ■ Hydrochloric acid | 200 mg |
| ■ Lutein | 10 mg |
| ■ Magnesium | 500 mg |
| ■ N-acetyl cysteine (NAC) | 500 mg |
| ■ Selenium | 200 mcg |

■ Taurine                    500 mg

■ Zinc                       30 mg

In most good health food stores you'll find shelves loaded with dozens of brands of vitamin-mineral products. Many of them have a multiple capsule specifically aimed at the eyes. Some are better than others.

Try for one which has the most of the above elements and at about the right total strength. You won't find any one that exactly matches the chart given above.

You may need to get a multivitamin that comes close, then get specific items such as Ginkgo biloba and garlic that few if any will have.

## How much is your sight worth?

Stupid question, but one you need to think about. Some of these supplements and vitamins are expensive. But think what an eye operation might cost, if there was one that would work. It might cost $15,000 to $840,000. Now look at the cost of the pills. Spending a relatively small amount each month for pills that could reverse, or at least stop, your macular degeneration doesn't sound like much at all. Will these pills work? Nobody can say for sure. Several ophthalmologists have reported that cases of macular degeneration have slowed and stopped when a regimen like the one on the chart above is followed. This is more often true for the less critical dry type of macular degeneration.

Will it work for you? I don't know.

I'm working on a six-month trial with near the above specifications of pills to see if it will work for me.

## A few more shots

Some last minute thoughts here. A 1994 study in the *Journal of the American Medical Association* cited the protective effects of carotenoids on macular degeneration.

These carotenoids are loaded with antioxidant properties. Beta-carotene is the best known. Researchers compared diets of 365 people with AMD against the diets of 520 with normal eyes. Everyone was over 55 years old. The group with the highest ingestion of carotenoids had the lowest incidence of macular degeneration, 43 percent lower than the other group.

The heavy hitters here were lutein and zeaxanthin. These two are found in bunches in dark green leafy vegetables: spinach, collard greens, kale, and beet greens. Beta-carotene here was not the winner, but it's also a good one to keep inside your diet prospectus.

A plug here for two more multivitamins designed for people with macular degeneration or cataracts: Icaps and Ocuvite. Both have a lot of what we need to resist AMD.

In a test, one-third of the folks with macular degeneration scored better on vision tests after taking the supplements for six months. The other test group showed that only 10 percent of the people not on the supplement scored better. Add to that the fact that 40 percent of the people in the non-supplement group continued to have deteriorating eyesight compared with only 22 percent of the people in the supplement group. Just a thought.

While we're talking beta-carotene, a Harvard Medical School study showed that people who ingest at least 8,700 IUs of beta-carotene a day had 50 percent less risk of developing macular degeneration than those getting less than that amount. Many one-a-day type multivitamin mineral tablets have 10,000 IU of beta-carotene in them. To add to this amount, eat carrots, broccoli, spinach, and apricots daily to boost your rating.

## Chromium

This mineral has been used to treat cataracts and macular degeneration. A man in Maryland says he completely reversed cataracts in their early stages with 200 mcg of chromium a day. We're not sure just how chromium works in the body, but it seems to affect everything! We do know that chromium absorption depends on other foods eaten during the same meal: greens help it, dairy products slow it down. Also when small amounts of chromium are added to a diet, the body uses vitamin C more efficiently.

## Pycnogenol

This is a trade name for an additive that's made from grapeseeds and the bark of the pine tree. It's a mixture of antioxidant molecules called by various names. Virtually the same thing is available as grapeseed extract. It is commonly available and about half the price of the trademarked item.

Pycnogenol is commonly called OPC, and is said to be outstanding for treating vascular diseases since it increases the structural strength of weakened blood vessels. It is also the most powerful antioxidant known—50 times as potent as vitamin E.

Antioxidants can help neutralize free radicals that cause so much trouble.

OPC has been used in Europe for 40 years, and it is said to be good for many problems.

OPC can help eyes recover from the glare of bright lights for better night vision. It is said to relieve eye stress caused by working at a computer for long hours.

Now doctors are saying that its strong antioxidant properties make it ideal for treating AMD. OPC tends to localize in the small vasculature of the eyes. This is especially good for wet macular degeneration where the weak blood cells leak.

A 200 mg tablet of OPC is a normal dose.

## Part of it's eating healthy

Ever snickered about people who demand organic grown fruits and vegetables? I have. "How much difference can it make?" I always asked.

Now, I'm rethinking.

The books I've read say that anything, (That's ANYTHING), you can do to get the best vitamins and minerals from your food and into your body, the better your body will be. That is especially important to the eyes.

So this simply means buy and use fresh vegetables whenever you can over those that are canned, boxed, or frozen.

We're talking a farmer's market in or near your home town. Even huge cities have them now. Get all of the fresh fruits and vegetables there that you can, and avoid the toxins, the pesticides, the sprays, and commercial fertilizers. Organic is better.

How do you know if it's organically grown? Most of the farmer's markets are up front about this. Some markets' management won't let an organic labeled grower in to sell until that grower proves the foods are organically grown.

You should also try to buy meat and fish that is hormone-, pesticide-, and drug-free. This is tougher to come by. It may take some digging. Much of the meat commercially produced today comes with growth hormones and antibiotics in it, fed by the farmers and ranchers for bigger yields.

So, what specific foods are good for your eyes?

- **Beta-carotene and vitamin A:** good sources are carrots, kale, collard greens, spinach, green leafy lettuce of all types, yams, broccoli, and Brussels sprouts, and many other vegetables and fruits. Remember, beta-carotene converts into vitamin A in the body, but you also want some A directly. While most of the vegetables are the same as those listed, you can add: peaches, tomatoes, squash, beet greens, cauliflower, and cabbage.

- **B vitamin group:** for the whole bunch of B vitamins look at brewer's yeast, whole grain cereals, and meat.

- **Calcium:** good sources here are all dairy products, soybean curd, broccoli, leafy green vegetables shown in the beta-carotene list above, almonds, and black-eyed peas.

- **Vitamin C:** this time it's all the citrus fruits oranges, limes, lemons, grapefruit, tangelos, and tangerines. Also mangoes, red peppers, tomatoes, and kiwis.

- **Vitamin D:** sunlight on your bare skin is one of the best ways to produce vitamin D in your body. The other is by what you eat including: cod liver oil and salmon.

- **Vitamin E:** tough one to get through food. Best is wheat germ and nuts of all kinds. Peanuts, sunflower seeds, walnuts, etc.

- **Chromium:** get it from these foods—liver, beef, brewer's yeast, whole wheat bread, beets, mushrooms, sugar beet molasses.

- **Copper:** almonds, whole grains, liver, green leafy vegetables mentioned before, dried peas, and beans, all kinds of seafood—salmon, scallops, crab, all sea-born fishes, mussels, prawns, oysters, clams.

- **Garlic:** get this from fresh garlic, the best way. About one clove a day...and breath mints.

- **Magnesium:** for this try wheat germ, soy, milk, whole grains, almonds and most nuts, seafood, figs, apples, corn, sunflower seeds, and pumpkin seeds.

- **Manganese:** egg yolks, whole grain cereal, all nuts and seeds, and all of the green leafy vegetables (about 10 of them).

- **Selenium:** meat and fish, brewer's yeast, fish and all shellfish, whole grains, all dairy products and cereals.

- **Zinc:** pumpkin seeds, whole grains, wheat bread, brewer's yeast, and wheat germ.

## Hey hey, it's a juicer!

One of the best ways to get your daily input of the good foods is with a juicer. These appliances take solids and turn them into juice, spitting out the fiber that can't be quickly liquefied.

They work amazingly well. Carrots for example. Wish you could get more beta-carotene but you're tired of crunching a carrot every noontime? You can put three medium sized carrots through a juicer and get a half-cup of juice and have more beta-carotene than you imagined.

A juicer is great for eating foods that you might not like. I can't stand the taste of greens, from spinach to collard greens. But once you put them through the juicer in combination with other compatible juices that you like, the taste doesn't become a factor. So you can get your daily input of leafy greens without a struggle.

Usually you don't mix fruits and vegetables in juice drinks, with the exception of the good old apple. The apple works well in almost every combination, from carrot-apple to the carrot-apple-cauliflower-parsley drink. Be careful or your parsley will slip through without getting juiced. You might want to juice it in combination with the apple or carrot.

What is good for the eyes in the juice field? Anything that is good for the eyes in the nutrition field. The green leafy veggies, and all the rest. It just might be easier for you to get your daily requirements of some of these vegetables and fruits that contain all of the vital nutrients that your eyes need. Give the juicer a try. You may get hooked and have made a new friend for life.

Here are some basic combinations of juices for the good of your eyes:

**Eye Clear:** 6 carrots and one handful of collard greens. This will make an 8-ounce cup of juice. You can vary this by using parsley or mustard greens or kale instead of the collard greens.

**Wake Up Eyes:** One grapefruit. Peel, leaving as much of the white pulp on as possible. Cut into sections and put through blender or juicer. Should make about 8 ounces of drink.

Try some of these simple juice mixes to give you lots of vitamins and minerals, and they even taste good, too:

- Carrot/apple juice: 6 carrots, 2 apples.
- Cantaloupe juice: cut cantaloupe with rind on into strips, and juice.

- Carrots/beet juice: three carrots and ½ beet.

- Pineapple juice: cut up pineapple, skin and all.

- Orange or Grapefruit: peel three oranges. Or peel one grapefruit.

- Apple/pear: two apples and one pear.

- Parsley/carrot: handful of parsley and 6 carrots.

- Spinach/parsley/celery/carrot juice: a handful of spinach, a handful of parsley, two stalks of celery, four carrots.

- Spinach/carrots: handful of spinach, six carrots.

- Celery/apple: 1 stalk of celery and two apples.

Hey, make up any combination you want to. Watermelon (with rind & seeds) juices well. Also cantaloupe with rinds and seeds. Have fun, and get healthier.

## Ten questions for your ophthalmologist

Some doctors will shy away from answering questions like these, others will be pleased to talk with you. Demand to get answers. These are your eyes we're talking about. They are yours, not the doctor's. Sit him down and get him to talk until you are satisfied you know everything you need to know about the state of your vision.

### Important Questions

1. What is the extent of the loss of my vision?

2. Would it help if I wore an eye patch over the affected eye while in the sun (if your AMD is in only one eye)?

❸ Why didn't you suggest a course of potent vitamins and supplements when you told me I had AMD?

❹ Do you think such an intense program can stop or slow down my AMD?

❺ How fast is my AMD progressing?

❻ If I'm 20 percent loss now, when might that go to 40, 60, or 80 percent?

❼ Do you think a vitamin-mineral supplement program can help prevent dry AMD from progressing to the wet type?

❽ Why did only one of my eyes get AMD?

❾ Will my other eye also develop AMD?

❿ How long does AMD develop in an eye before a patient realizes something is wrong?

# 4 Drugs That Can Damage Your Eyes

Most of us take some kind of medication more often than we should. Over-the-counter pills such as pain relievers: Advil, Tylenol, Motrin. We go to the doctor and get a prescription he says will be good for us, and we take it with few questions. Some of us take the same prescription for years on end, without thinking to check with the doctor to see if we still really need it.

Do this: If you are from 50 to 80 years old, chances are that you are taking from three to five prescription pills daily. Yes, I know, each has a purpose and fills a need.

How long has it been since the medication was first prescribed? Do you still need it? Give your doctor a call and ask about each of your prescriptions. If you have macular degeneration, tell him or her and find out if your medication is having any effect on your eyes. There's no sense being perfectly healthy and blind.

This little review of your medical history and current intake could be a benefit to you whether any of your current prescription medications infringe on the macula or not.

## Drugs that hurt your eyes

Plaquenil, hydroxchloroquine sulfate, is a drug that is routinely prescribed by rheumatologists for rheumatoid arthritis. It shouldn't be.

Plaquenil has caused irreversible retinal damage in many people across the country. In many health groups, a follow-up by the optometry department each six months is mandatory for anyone who is taking Plaquenil. It can cause a buildup on the retina, and the optometrists are supposed to watch out for this.

I have been taking Plaquenil for the past three years. I don't know if the Plaquenil was the primary cause of my macular degeneration, or if it only assisted. My AMD was found by an optometrist at one of these six-month checkups. Why wasn't it caught earlier? I don't know. Even with the best intentions, records are not always complete.

Many older people have rheumatoid arthritis. Plaquenil does a good job of eliminating the pain from the arthritis. But is it worth it? There must be another medication that can do the job and not cause me to go blind. I'm having a good long talk with my rheumatologist, and we'll go over the problem in minute detail. As I asked him, "What good is perfectly working, able-to-type hands, if I'm blind?"

Are you now taking Plaquenil? If so, get an appointment quickly and see if you can get another medication. If I had my way I would ban Plaquenil.

## Other bad medications

These drugs can also damage the retina. Clonidine, brand name Catapres. This is a drug used to lower your blood pressure. Thioridazine. This one fights infections but can cause pigmentary retinopathy.

The whole family of NSAIDs (nonsteroidal anti-inflammatory drugs) can create problems with the eyes. These include aspirin, ibuprofen (Advil, Motrin), flurbiprofen, ketoprofen, and naproxen sodium. While it is not an NSAID, acetaminophen (Tylenol) is not completely risk-free either, because it affects the liver in surprising ways. Check with your doctor.

## Eye hemorrhage can be caused by these drugs

- NSAIDs, over-the-counter pain relievers
- Venlafaxine, an antidepressant
- Amphotericin B, which is an antibiotic
- Cholinesterase inhibitors, often used for Alzheimer's
- Pentoxifylline, for blood clotting
- Heparin, coumadin, anisidione, oral anticoagulants

## These drugs can cause glaucoma or damage the optic nerve

- NSAIDs
- Venlafaxine
- Glucocorticoids (Prednisone)
- Simvastatin
- Fenfluramine
- Mirtazapine
- Gastric antispasmodics.

## These drugs can worsen or cause cataracts

- NSAIDs
- Fluroquinone, terbinafine, mefloquine-type antibiotics.
- Glucocorticoids (Prednisone)
- Eretinate, isoretinoin.

## Two drugs that can cause blood clotting, harm blood flow to the eyes

- Androgen replacement with synthetic hormones.
- Estrogen (Premarin)

## Generally speaking about drugs

Some over-prescribed and overused drugs you might be able to replace.

NSAIDs. Yes, generally too many people use too much aspirin and ibuprofen. These are Advil, Motrin, Bayer, and Aleve.

These harmless looking drugs do have side effects. When used in excess they can produce photosensitivity, dry eyes, corneal deposits, gastrointestinal tract damage, and even cause cataracts. Don't use these drugs unless you feel you absolutely must. You might ask your doctor for some safer form of pain relief or tissue repair drug.

Cortisone prescriptions, such as Prednisone, do the most damage to the eye of any prescription drugs. This type of drug is used for patients with arthritis, asthma, skin disorders, and autoimmune diseases.

If it is mandatory that you take one of these corticosteroids, be sure to take the highest doses of antioxidants such as vitamins E and C, and beta-carotene. They will help control the damage. Better yet, find a substitute drug to replace the Prednisone. One source said hydrocortisone, a natural cortisone, might work just as well as Prednisone without the danger to the eyes.

Two other classes of drugs that are over-prescribed and overused are antibiotics and diuretics, which can disrupt the natural chemistry and fluid balance of the eyes.

# 5 Take Care of Your Eyes

L et's take a look at some of the steps you can take to maintain healthy eyes. It isn't so hard.

## Sunglasses

The most obvious way to protect your eyes is with a good pair of sunglasses. Exposure to bright light—high levels or sudden flashes—may aggravate macular degeneration.

The basic requirement for sunglasses is that they should block out 100 percent of Ultra Violet A (UV-A) and Ultra Violet B (UV-B) rays. These are the guys that damage your eye and cause oxidation in the retina which messes up everything. This oxidation is suspected to be a prime cause of both macular degeneration and cataracts.

Estimates are that fully half of the sunglasses sold today do more harm than good for your eyes. Even those sunshades that claim to be good for 100 percent on both of the UV rays probably are telling the truth only half the time. The problem is it's hard to test glasses, and usually we have to take some salesperson's word for it.

Part of the solution here is to buy your sunglasses from a permanent sunglass or optical company that is going to be around for a while. Those $2.95 specials at the gasoline station cash register probably are worth about that much.

So, what should you look for in a good pair of sunshades?

- Buy from a recognized store. It has to be sure of the quality of the sunglasses it sells or the place will go out of business.

- The lenses must be able to block out 100 percent of both UV-A and UV-B rays. How can you be sure? Some stores provide an ultraviolet light sensor. This is simply a card that will fit in your wallet. You take the sunglasses outside and let the sun shine through them and onto the card. If the card changes color, UV rays are getting through.

  What you need to know about UV rays: They are invisible. The rays don't make your eyes hurt, say like sunburned skin does. The UV rays don't even feel hot on your skin. Remember that the UV rays are there on cloudy days, because they go right through the clouds. Does the time of day matter? Yes. UV rays are strongest from (regular time not daylight savings) 10 a.m. to 2 p.m. This will differ in other sections of the world. Check local danger times. Is there anything good about UV rays? Yes. Short-term exposure manufactures vitamin D in your skin. But this can be gained in 10 to 15 minutes of sunshine a day.

- What color lens? A darker lens will let in less light, but not necessarily fewer UV rays. The darker lenses can also make it hard to see in late afternoon and could be the cause of an accident. There are many shades of lenses. One popular one is the gray, since it doesn't change the colors of what you see. The orange/ brown lenses are best if you have macular degeneration. These filter out the UV rays and 75 percent of the blue rays. Green lenses give you a more natural color spread and many people like them. On the other hand, yellow lenses may help reduce glare, especially for those with contact lenses. Most good sunshades made today come with lightweight plastic lenses. If you're a sport nut you can get shatterproof ones as well. Glass lenses usually are too heavy for most people's tastes.

- Polarization? Yes, if you want it. Though polarization doesn't help protect your eyes, it can help you see better in extremely bright light.

- Blue light? Mentioned it above. Blue light rays in normal sunlight are murder on your eyes. The rays react with pigment deposits on the retina and make free radicals, which cause retinal damage. Many experts think that blue light alone can result in enough damage over the years to produce macular degeneration. The Schepens Eye Research Institute demonstrated that the blue rays of the spectrum accelerate macular degeneration—blocking them may decrease the rate.

- How to check your sunshades? If you look at a blue sky through your sunglasses and the sky appears a light shade of gray, your lenses are filtering out a lot of the blue rays. Keep the shades.

- Those mirrored glasses some people wear? Don't bother. They may keep you from being recognized, but the shades usually don't filter out any of the UV rays.

- A hat? You bet. The bigger the brim the better. Baseball type hats worm with the bill to the front are good, as are Western hats, straw hats with big brims and yes, even a good old fedora.

## Tears and your eyes

What are those tears that come out of your eyes once in a while and roll down your cheeks besides slightly salty water?

Tears are for a lot more than crying. The fact is tears are made up of three "layers." The first one is a fatty layer that slides along between the inner two layers and the outside world. This one is slightly fatty so water can't evaporate through it. Otherwise your eyes would dry up.

The center layer of this trio is mainly made of water. The inner layer that flows across your eyeball contains mucin, which actually helps to spread your tears across the surface of your eyeball every time you blink. Those same tears also have a special type of enzyme that helps to kill airborne bacteria. Put the package together and your tears help keep your eye protected, lubricated, and working all day long.

Where does this complicated formula come from? Small glands in your eyelids produce these enzymes, oils, and mucins. Every time you blink, more of the fluid is secreted to keep your eye working properly. The water that goes along with these three comes from the lacrimal glands situated slightly below your brow. These glands produce extra water to mix with the special fluids when you run into smoke or dust, or just start to cry.

Sometimes these lacrimal glands stop working. It can happen to people who have rheumatoid arthritis, childhood diabetes, and lupus.

So what can you do if you have dry eyes? Your job is to restore the film that keeps the water against your eyeball to working order instead of evaporating.

Omega-3 fatty acids from fish and fish oil will be helpful. Omega-6 fatty acids will help with the lipid layer.

Vitamin C is another good help here. The natural tear film on the eye has a high concentration of vitamin C. You'll want to drink plenty of water to improve the watery layer of the tears. Oh, and you might want to cut down or cut out drinking coffee, which can make the dry eye problem worse.

If you really have a bad case of dry eye, a doctor might prescribe the supplement glucosamine sulfate. This is a natural substance that will help rebuild the collagen matrix of the cornea.

Blinking often is good for your eyes. It helps bring more fluid and spreads it over your naked eyeball. Your eyes are the most vulnerable part of the human body. They are sitting out there in the dirt and grit of everyday living with only a few tears to protect them. Help things along all you can.

Oh, if you work at a computer the way I do, try to position the screen so it is slightly below eye level. This means that you will be looking down a little at the screen, which will make it easier on your eyes.

Now for something a little strange. Since tears are secreted when you blink, the whole process stops at night when you go to sleep. No blinking, so no tears and your tear glands take a long nap themselves.

Sometimes your eyes may not close all the way when you go to sleep. It happens. The body rushes a protein material to the eye to cover the open part so your eye won't dry out as you snore.

If you wake up with some bits and pieces of "sticky stuff" in the corner of your eye, that's what has happened.

That's normal and don't worry about it. But, if you have a lot of it and it's stringy and you have trouble opening your eyes in the morning, it's time for you to go see your ophthalmologist. He may suggest that you tape your eyes closed when you go to sleep. Yeah, true, no kidding.

Now, back to these dry eyes. The dry eye problem might be coming from medications you are taking. Check with your doctor and see if any of them could be reacting this way on you. Artificial tears sold over-the-counter will give you temporary relief but will not solve the problem.

Some experts say poor nutrition and hormone imbalances may be the leading causes of dry eyes. Not getting enough essential fatty acids or vitamins A, B-6, and C can affect the sensitive lubrication system we talked about above. The solution here is to bring your intake of these vitamins up to the minimum daily standard and more until the problem is solved.

Dry eyes can be caused by an imbalance of the hormones estrogen or progesterone. Dry eyes can also be caused by allergies. Some women have trouble when they use new eye makeup. If this happens, drop off one new eye product at a time for a week or two until you find the culprit and quit using that one.

## What about eye drops?

The use of eye drops becomes more prevalent as a person gets older. This can present a problem. Arthritis, just poor aim, and shaking hands trying to use the dropper, can all be a handicap in the eye drop game. Even uncontrolled blinking which leaves the medication running down the outside of your cheeks doesn't help.

Short course in eye drop use. The best way is to follow directions on the label. Most say:

- Pull down the lower lid of your eye with one hand and with the other squeeze the required drops into the place between the lower lid and the eyeball.

- You should look upward just before putting in the drops.

- Be careful not to touch the eyedropper tip to any part of the eye or eyelid.

- After the drops are safely inside your eye, close your eye, then roll your eye from side to side and up and down to get the medication distributed evenly where it should be. By closing your eye, you'll keep the medicine inside, where it belongs.

You say you still can't get the goods in the eye? Try the second method, the lying down one.

Lie down and put the needed drops on the inner corner of your closed eye. Then open that eye so the drops will drain into your eye. Then when they are safely where they should be, close your eye and move it around as before. You may need someone to help you do this.

This is the ideal way to put drops in a child's eye. Children are notoriously afraid of anything being put in their eyes.

Some more tips. If your brand of eye drops sting when they go in, keep the supply in the refrigerator. The coldness will help numb the eye just enough to negate the stinging.

If you must use an ointment, say after surgery, use it AFTER your eye drops. You may wish to warm the ointment container by holding it in your hand for a few minutes.

To put the ointment in your eye, pull out the lower lid and put the ointment on the inside edge of the eyelid. Then release the eyelid and let it close. Keeping your eye closed, move it around as you did with the eye drops and that will distribute the ointment over your eyeball.

# 6 Your Eyes and Acupressure and Reflexology

While there is little that either acupressure or reflexology can do to help you specifically with the condition of macular degeneration, some procedures might help you with your eyes in general.

Yes, both of these methods of treating the body are on the fringes of medical science. However, as a wise man I once knew said "If it works, use it. Don't worry about what the source is."

For many people acupressure and reflexology are methods that work for them. Both of these systems are based on the idea that energy flows freely in a healthy body. Any interruption in the flow can be corrected by applying specific pressure to corresponding areas of the body to restore the circulation. Here are the vital elements of some of these treatments that could help your eyes. They might work for you.

## Acupressure

If you have eyestrain, you may be able to relieve the problem by the use of acupressure. This isn't going to do anything for your AMD, but it can't hurt.

Many things can cause eyestrain from reading to watching too much TV or working too long on a computer. When your eyes feel strained, it's usually a signal that your whole body is fatigued. Your eyestrain might be accompanied by a headache and tension in the back of your neck and shoulders.

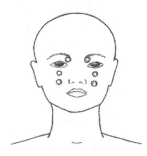

Try these:

Put your thumbs on the upper ridge of your eye sockets close to the bridge of your nose. Then gently press upward into the indentations of the eye sockets. Hold this position for one minute as you breathe deeply.

Then put your index fingers in the center of your cheeks below the lower ridge of your eyes and in line with your eye's pupil. Now, position your middle finger directly below your index fingers under the cheekbones. Close your eyes and apply light pressure on the points and breathe deeply for a minute.

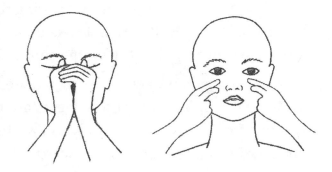

The third step to relieve eyestrain by acupressure is to put your fingers on the ropy muscles that run parallel to your spine up the back of your neck. Press firmly and hold for one minute. During this time, breathe deeply.

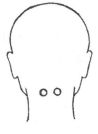

# Reflexology

This might work for you, and it might not. Don't write it off simply because to you it seems to have no medical or logical basis. Give it try.

For health and comfort of the eyes:

Use your left thumb to press on the first bend of the right index finger. Make small clockwise rotating movements with your thumb without exerting too much pressure. Repeat this pressure rotation three times for 10 seconds each.

Now holding your left hand straight, use your right thumb and work up the thumb to the top, then repeat the pressure on each of the fingers from tip to base. After working your left hand, use your left thumb and do the same to the right thumb and fingers.

This work is especially suited to help in recovery from conjunctivitis and is aimed at the sinus area.

Hold your right foot with your left hand. Put your right thumb under the first bend of the second toe. Now make small rotating movements in a clockwise direction. Repeat the same procedure on the left foot.

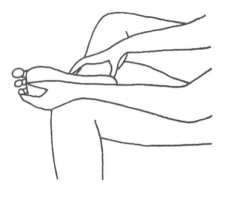

Another exercise to work the sinus cavities is this one:

Support your right foot with your left hand. With your right thumb, work up all of the toes with small swift strokes. Start at the base of the big toe. Be sure to treat the whole surface of each toe. When finished, do the same work on the other foot.

For glaucoma, reflexology may reduce the pain. Treatments can help cut down the pressure involved. Daily treatments may prove helpful in cutting down on the pain. Again, use the same treatment as for the sinus area detailed above.

# 7

# Exercise to Help Your Eyes

Read that line again. Exercise to help your eyes. Sounds a bit peculiar, doesn't it? I don't mean actually exercising your eyes themselves, I mean getting your body enough exercise that it helps to pump enough blood through the old veins that the eyes are going to benefit from that increased blood flow.

Fact: The better an exercise program you have to keep your body moving and to keep it in as fit a condition as it should be for your age, the more benefit your eyes will derive from that exercise.

Blood flow. I'm talking about aerobic exercises here. Yes, free weights are fine, if you're 20 or 30. At 50 or 60 or 70, we don't have a great need for a lot of hairy muscle mass. Pumping iron isn't the way to go—in fact, straining can cause small eye vessels to rupture.

What's a good aerobic exercise? The best one is walking, because it's the easiest to do, takes no equipment or even a partner, and you can do it anytime anywhere.

Walking?

Right. If you've been holding down the couch cushions lately with a steady diet of TV, now is the time to get off your gluteus maximus and get some exercise. That blood pumping through your arteries will carry all sorts of good antioxidants and oxygen to your eyes and help kill off the bad cells.

One word of caution. No matter what your age, from 20 to 80, you should go to your general practitioner or family physician for a physical checkup before you begin any form of exercise program. Well, you can probably do the walking without your doctor's approval, but it wouldn't hurt. No sense in being a perfectly physically fit corpse.

## How much, how far?

Let's say the most walking you've done lately is to the bathroom, then to the kitchen, and maybe one circle around the shopping mall. So, you're starting from square one.

Give it a try the first day in the morning or the evening when the weather is the least extreme. Do a four-block circuit and wind up back at your house or condo. Walk at a rate that you feel comfortable with and that you can maintain. If it's an out and back route, remember it will always take you longer to cover the same distance when you come back. You're getting a little tired.

How do you feel? If you're not even breathing hard, put another two blocks with it, one away from home and another back to home base. This "circuit" idea gives you a stopping point every so often if you get tired.

Say you did six blocks yesterday, and today you feel a little bit stiff in your hips and elbows. How bad? Not enough to keep you off the sidewalks again. Good. Try the same six blocks again. Do them daily or three times a week, until you can do the circuit without feeling sore or stiff.

Forget the untruth "No pain, no gain." That might be workable for weight lifters, but not for us amateurs in the exercising department.

When you find you easily can do the six blocks or nearly a half mile go another two to four blocks, again in the circuit pattern so you pass your house twice on the routine. Then if something goes wrong, or you get excessively tired, you can bail out and do the rest of your workout sitting on the porch swing.

An ideal length of time for you to exercise is half an hour a day. The length of time is more important than the distance. During this time your heart will be pumping away at an increased rate. This will strengthen it, giving it more reserve power if and when you need it.

In addition to increasing your heart rate, the exercise will elevate your blood pressure. Both drive blood through every capillary in your body, especially those areas in your eyes where a good blood supply, with plenty of antioxidants in it, is vital to your eyes' good health.

Most adults who are not wheelchair—or bed-bound get exercise doing daily chores such as cleaning the house, mowing the lawn, working in the garden, even doing the laundry, and cooking meals.

This exercise, plus a good half-hour of walking, should be enough to keep you on the plus side of the ledger for good blood circulation.

If you want more than a walking program, or just a different one, there are other kinds of aerobics that work just as well. Swimming for 20 minutes a day is an excellent workout. Swimming has been called the perfect exercise, since it causes the least wear and tear on the body. Even with walking there is a pounding of the feet against the ground. With swimming there is no sudden jarring effect on the body.

Bicycling is another good aerobic workout. Be cautious where you ride. If you're in traffic, remember that many drivers will look right at you and never realize you are in the way. You must ride defensively at all times and be ready to steer quickly out of the way of some driver who thinks you're a pole, post, or somebody far off the roadway.

Other types of aerobic exercise include cross-country skiing, jogging, and even ballroom dancing.

The other popular form of aerobics is the organized, gym-type aerobic group dancing. This bouncing, jumping, always on-the-move type of exercise can be tremendously difficult and hard on your body. Check with your doctor before you start any type of exercise like this.

Pick out an exercise that you can do every day, or every other day, and keep at it. The more the aerobic the exercise, the better your body will function overall. The more rich red blood will be pumped into your system to flush those cell tips out of your retina and to do all the other vital services blood does.

If you want more, there are all types of exercise programs you can use. The simplest of all is the homestyle free weight workout. For this all you need are two weights from two to 10 pounds. You can then do curl-ups with the weights, lift them over your head, drop them behind you and lift them again, or use them on your ankles as you do leg lifts.

You can also do free exercises such as push-ups, lunges, jumping jacks, or running in place.

Again, less is more here. Start out gradually with one or two exercises you used to do. Give it a try. Can you still do them? If you aren't stiff and sore after the first few days, add another exercise to your list.

Some retirement communities have organized exercise and walking programs. You might get into one of those, so you can have company as you go through your workout. Sometimes the camaraderie is as important as the exercises.

# What about calorie burn off?

Most people these days are worried about being overweight. This comes back to the basic principle of the human body. If you take in more calories than your body burns off, you will put on weight. If you take in fewer calories than you burn off, you will lose weight.

We've talked some about the importance of a good diet in conjunction with your eyesight. Now you can double up that good diet with an exercise program that will help keep your blood circulating and at the same time can help you lose weight.

That hamburger at the fast food place is not the way to lose weight. Fast food hamburgers have an amazing number of calories and fat. Check out the calorie and fat counter in the appendix.

How many calories can you burn off by exercising for 15 minutes?

Here is a burn off chart:

## Exercise Calories burned in 15 minutes

| Exercise | Calories |
|---|---|
| Walking 3 mph | 65 |
| Walking 4 mph | 100 |
| Walking up stairs | 150 |
| Walking up hills | 125 |
| Aerobic dancing | 100 |
| Bicycling at 6 mph | 70 |
| Bicycling at 10 mph | 105 |
| Stationary exercise bike | 70 |
| Running at 12 minutes per mile | 143 |
| Running at 8 minutes per mile | 215 |
| Running at 6 minutes per mile | 260 |
| Rowing machine fast | 110 |
| Nordic Track machine | 150 |
| Swimming the crawl stroke | 145 |
| Stair climber machine | 155 |
| Treadmill at moderate speed | 120 |

Look over the chart. You'll quickly see that it's tremendously easier not to eat a 150 calorie dessert than it is to work it off by walking up stairs for 15 minutes.

## How can exercising help your lifestyle?

A program of regular exercise can do a lot of good things for your body and your life.

- Your heart will get stronger with your exercise and be able to stand up better under any physical challenges. As your heart gets stronger, it's like a big engine that has to work less to keep your vehicle moving smoothly down the road.

- If you're a diabetic, you probably will be able to cut down on your insulin.

- Your blood circulation is improved, which also means a stronger blood flow to your eyes with all of those antioxidants you have been eating.

- There should be a reduction in your bad blood fats, and at the same time your good cholesterol (HDL) should increase.

- Your high blood pressure should be coming down a little as you continue your exercising.

- For most of you, you'll be able to sleep better as you exercise more.

- Soon you'll have more energy with your exercising, partly due to the better diet you'll desire.

- Exercise helps to build up your immune system to fight infections and diseases.

■ Even your breathing will become deeper and in greater volume as you continue to work out on your aerobic exercises.

■ A walking program will help keep your bones strong and resistant to problems like osteoporosis.

So, when are you going to start your exercise program? Remember, it's mainly for your eyes, but there are also a lot of secondary benefits. Why not set up a beginning walking schedule, make out a chart to check off every day you do it, and get moving.

## Exercise Chart

Here is a chart made out and ready for you. Start with the month it is today and the day. Simply put a check below every day that you do your exercises, no matter what they are. It might be a walk, or a swim, or dancing.

Remember, it will be best if you check with your doctor before starting any exercise program.

Now, get it moving!

| January | | | | | | | | | | | | | | | | | | | | | | | | | | | | | | |
|---|---|---|---|---|---|---|---|---|---|---|---|---|---|---|---|---|---|---|---|---|---|---|---|---|---|---|---|---|---|---|
| 1 | 2 | 3 | 4 | 5 | 6 | 7 | 8 | 9 | 10 | 11 | 12 | 13 | 14 | 15 | 16 | 17 | 18 | 19 | 20 | 21 | 22 | 23 | 24 | 25 | 26 | 27 | 28 | 29 | 30 | 31 |
|  |  |  |  |  |  |  |  |  |  |  |  |  |  |  |  |  |  |  |  |  |  |  |  |  |  |  |  |  |  |  |

| February | | | | | | | | | | | | | | | | | | | | | | | | | | | | |
|---|---|---|---|---|---|---|---|---|---|---|---|---|---|---|---|---|---|---|---|---|---|---|---|---|---|---|---|---|
| 1 | 2 | 3 | 4 | 5 | 6 | 7 | 8 | 9 | 10 | 11 | 12 | 13 | 14 | 15 | 16 | 17 | 18 | 19 | 20 | 21 | 22 | 23 | 24 | 25 | 26 | 27 | 28 | 29 |
|  |  |  |  |  |  |  |  |  |  |  |  |  |  |  |  |  |  |  |  |  |  |  |  |  |  |  |  |  |  |

| March | | | | | | | | | | | | | | | | | | | | | | | | | | | | | | |
|---|---|---|---|---|---|---|---|---|---|---|---|---|---|---|---|---|---|---|---|---|---|---|---|---|---|---|---|---|---|---|---|
| 1 | 2 | 3 | 4 | 5 | 6 | 7 | 8 | 9 | 10 | 11 | 12 | 13 | 14 | 15 | 16 | 17 | 18 | 19 | 20 | 21 | 22 | 23 | 24 | 25 | 26 | 27 | 28 | 29 | 30 | 31 |
|  |  |  |  |  |  |  |  |  |  |  |  |  |  |  |  |  |  |  |  |  |  |  |  |  |  |  |  |  |  |  |  |  |

## April

| 1 | 2 | 3 | 4 | 5 | 6 | 7 | 8 | 9 | 10 | 11 | 12 | 13 | 14 | 15 | 16 | 17 | 18 | 19 | 20 | 21 | 22 | 23 | 24 | 25 | 26 | 27 | 28 | 29 | 30 | |
|---|---|---|---|---|---|---|---|---|---|---|---|---|---|---|---|---|---|---|---|---|---|---|---|---|---|---|---|---|---|---|
| | | | | | | | | | | | | | | | | | | | | | | | | | | | | | | |

## May

| 1 | 2 | 3 | 4 | 5 | 6 | 7 | 8 | 9 | 10 | 11 | 12 | 13 | 14 | 15 | 16 | 17 | 18 | 19 | 20 | 21 | 22 | 23 | 24 | 25 | 26 | 27 | 28 | 29 | 30 | 31 |
|---|---|---|---|---|---|---|---|---|---|---|---|---|---|---|---|---|---|---|---|---|---|---|---|---|---|---|---|---|---|---|
| | | | | | | | | | | | | | | | | | | | | | | | | | | | | | | |

## June

| 1 | 2 | 3 | 4 | 5 | 6 | 7 | 8 | 9 | 10 | 11 | 12 | 13 | 14 | 15 | 16 | 17 | 18 | 19 | 20 | 21 | 22 | 23 | 24 | 25 | 26 | 27 | 28 | 29 | 30 | |
|---|---|---|---|---|---|---|---|---|---|---|---|---|---|---|---|---|---|---|---|---|---|---|---|---|---|---|---|---|---|---|---|
| | | | | | | | | | | | | | | | | | | | | | | | | | | | | | | |

## July

| 1 | 2 | 3 | 4 | 5 | 6 | 7 | 8 | 9 | 10 | 11 | 12 | 13 | 14 | 15 | 16 | 17 | 18 | 19 | 20 | 21 | 22 | 23 | 24 | 25 | 26 | 27 | 28 | 29 | 30 | 31 |
|---|---|---|---|---|---|---|---|---|---|---|---|---|---|---|---|---|---|---|---|---|---|---|---|---|---|---|---|---|---|---|---|
| | | | | | | | | | | | | | | | | | | | | | | | | | | | | | | |

## August

| 1 | 2 | 3 | 4 | 5 | 6 | 7 | 8 | 9 | 10 | 11 | 12 | 13 | 14 | 15 | 16 | 17 | 18 | 19 | 20 | 21 | 22 | 23 | 24 | 25 | 26 | 27 | 28 | 29 | 30 | 31 |
|---|---|---|---|---|---|---|---|---|---|---|---|---|---|---|---|---|---|---|---|---|---|---|---|---|---|---|---|---|---|---|---|
| | | | | | | | | | | | | | | | | | | | | | | | | | | | | | | |

## September

| 1 | 2 | 3 | 4 | 5 | 6 | 7 | 8 | 9 | 10 | 11 | 12 | 13 | 14 | 15 | 16 | 17 | 18 | 19 | 20 | 21 | 22 | 23 | 24 | 25 | 26 | 27 | 28 | 29 | 30 | |
|---|---|---|---|---|---|---|---|---|---|---|---|---|---|---|---|---|---|---|---|---|---|---|---|---|---|---|---|---|---|---|---|
| | | | | | | | | | | | | | | | | | | | | | | | | | | | | | | |

## October

| 1 | 2 | 3 | 4 | 5 | 6 | 7 | 8 | 9 | 10 | 11 | 12 | 13 | 14 | 15 | 16 | 17 | 18 | 19 | 20 | 21 | 22 | 23 | 24 | 25 | 26 | 27 | 28 | 29 | 30 | 31 |
|---|---|---|---|---|---|---|---|---|---|---|---|---|---|---|---|---|---|---|---|---|---|---|---|---|---|---|---|---|---|---|---|
| | | | | | | | | | | | | | | | | | | | | | | | | | | | | | | |

## November

| 1 | 2 | 3 | 4 | 5 | 6 | 7 | 8 | 9 | 10 | 11 | 12 | 13 | 14 | 15 | 16 | 17 | 18 | 19 | 20 | 21 | 22 | 23 | 24 | 25 | 26 | 27 | 28 | 29 | 30 | |
|---|---|---|---|---|---|---|---|---|---|---|---|---|---|---|---|---|---|---|---|---|---|---|---|---|---|---|---|---|---|---|---|
| | | | | | | | | | | | | | | | | | | | | | | | | | | | | | | |

## December

| 1 | 2 | 3 | 4 | 5 | 6 | 7 | 8 | 9 | 10 | 11 | 12 | 13 | 14 | 15 | 16 | 17 | 18 | 19 | 20 | 21 | 22 | 23 | 24 | 25 | 26 | 27 | 28 | 29 | 30 | 31 |
|---|---|---|---|---|---|---|---|---|---|---|---|---|---|---|---|---|---|---|---|---|---|---|---|---|---|---|---|---|---|---|---|
| | | | | | | | | | | | | | | | | | | | | | | | | | | | | | | |

CHAPTER

# Cataracts

If you know anyone 60 or 70 years old, you probably know about cataracts. This eye condition affects two out of three persons who are over 70 years of age.

What is a cataract? This is a condition of the lens of the eye. With aging, the lens loses its flexibility. Unlike most of the body, there is no cell replacement in the eye lens. The one you're born with is supposed to last for your lifetime. It always used to. Now people are living longer, and more people experience cataracts.

Most cataracts are caused by poor nutrition, sugar accumulating in the eye's lens, and intense exposure to the sun. It might develop from one or all of these causes.

Antioxidants seem to play an important part in preventing cata-

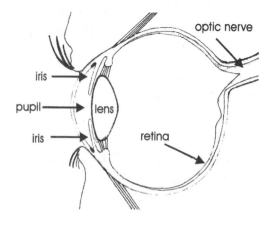

racts. Proteins give the lens of the eye its transparency. This makes it the only clear organ in the body. These proteins are called crystallins. When the eye is damaged by chronic exposure to the sun's ultraviolet rays, free radicals form, and the crystallins clump together. This is thought to be what makes the eye lens opaque resulting in a cataract.

Antioxidants could have a big part in preventing the crystallins from clumping by attacking the free radicals. More on this later.

The older we get, the less light passes normally through the lenses. This means also that we're seeing less than we did before. Some say that at age 65 only 40 percent of the light that hits the lens passes through to the retina.

A short footnote here. With less sunlight passing through the lens to the retina, the cataract is actually shielding the eye from the sun's rays and helping to slow or prevent macular degeneration.

Cataracts sneak up on you. You may think that you're getting older and you don't see as well as you used to, so you must need new glasses. You probably do, but you also could be developing cataracts. The lens in the eye is less than a quarter of an inch thick. As it gets older, it thickens and becomes inflexible so it can't focus, as it needs to for good sight.

Everything can look fuzzy or hazy, and again it seems like new glasses are needed. The lens can also turn a soft shade of yellow and disrupt normal color vision. The lack of good vision can result in falls and blurring that would prevent driving.

Diabetics are prone to cataracts due to the excess sugar in their blood. This makes their eyes' lenses swell up and become less than transparent. Heavy smokers and people who live in sunny climates are also more prone to cataracts than nonsmokers and those who live in cloudy climates.

## How do you treat cataracts?

The surgical removal and replacement of the eye lens is a common procedure these days. It is highly effective and relatively simple. Recovery time is short.

The latest in technology for lens removal is a procedure called phacoemulsification. The lens is held in place in a thin capsule. This procedure inserts a small tube powered by a vacuum into the eye. It ultrasonically shatters the diseased lens and pulls the particles out of the capsule. When all the fragments are removed, a new lens is inserted into the capsule and it is closed.

The operation is quick and simple, and some surgeons prefer to do both eyes at the same time if there is a need. The harm done to the eye is minor, and the patient is seeing well within a short time.

The lens of your eye helps you focus, so when it has to be removed, it usually is replaced. There are three types of lenses that can be used.

## Intraocular lens (IOL)

The IOL is a clear, plastic lens that goes in your eye during cataract surgery. It requires no care by you, the new owner. You'll have better vision and won't feel or see the new lens. About 90 percent of people who get replacement lenses use the IOL. With it they can achieve 20/40 vision, which isn't bad.

Some people can't use the plastic lens because their eyes won't tolerate the material the lens is made of or their eyes' structure isn't suitable.

## Contact lenses

Most patients who don't get the IOL use soft contact lenses instead. Extended wear lenses are helpful especially if you have trouble putting them in and taking them out. As with any contact lens, it's important to pay special attention to the instructions about care and use.

## Cataract glasses

Some people don't want to use contact lenses or their eyes are too sensitive to wear them. For these people, cataract glasses are a choice. These are not regular eyeglasses. They have powerful magnification of 20 to 35 percent and may make it hard for the wearer to judge distance and also will change side vision until you get used to them. So at first, be careful.

The latest development in lenses is to make them with ultraviolet light filters. These then help protect the eye from the harmful rays that may cause macular degeneration.

After lens implants, the patient is told to wear good UV protection sunglasses whenever going outside. A hat with a brim is also a good idea, even if your new lenses have the ultraviolet filter.

## Sneaking up on you

Again, the very nature of the clouding of the lens of your eyes means that you probably won't be aware that anything is wrong until the cataracts have advanced. A good way to discover cataracts is to have a yearly eye examination by a qualified optometrist or ophthalmologist.

Sometimes early-forming cataracts are found before the person senses anything wrong. They are not severe enough to warrant removal. The doctor watches their development and when the time is right the operation is performed. At least this way the patient knows there is a problem, and he or she can be especially careful not to fall or to drive when it isn't advised.

## How will you know that you might have cataracts?

- Bad color choices. If you can't tell for sure which socks go with which pants.

- Double vision. You see two of everything where there should be only one.

- If vision is brighter for one eye than the other. Check this by closing one eye and watching closely. Then change eyes and compare the brightness.

- Are you having your eyeglasses changed frequently?

- If the sun seems to glare into your eyes without reason.

- Difficulty in reading, watching TV, or participating in normal activities.

- If you have one eye that doesn't follow the other one as quickly as it should.

If you notice some or all of these problems, you should make an appointment to see your eye doctor as soon as possible.

## Can you prevent cataracts?

There are several things you can do that may help prevent the formulation of cataracts.

Keep the harmful sun's rays from your eyes. Do this by always wearing good UV-proof sunglasses whenever you are outside on a sunny or partly cloudy day. Be sure to wear a hat with a wide brim or a bill cap with the bill out in front to help shield your eyes.

Much of what you learned about helping to prevent macular degeneration works for cataracts as well. Get a good diet loaded with spinach, eggs, asparagus, garlic, carrots, onions, cantaloupes, yams, corn, and all kinds of greens, collard to spinach.

Also include in your diet sea vegetables, celery, citrus fruits, brewer's yeast, sprouts, apples and apple juice, legumes, and a daily shot of carrot juice.

Increase your intake of seeds such as sunflower, almonds, whole grains, wheat germ, and wheat germ oil. These are all good sources of antioxidants and vitamin E.

An old folk remedy calls for you to drink two ounces of green bean juice three times a day. You'll want to cut this with a milder tomato or carrot juice.

Then be sure to avoid foods that generate free radicals such as fried, smoked, and barbecued foods. Rancid foods and oils should always be avoided.

## Special juices to help foil cataracts

- Carrot, kale, parsley and spinach: beta-carotene.
- Garlic juice: vitamin B-1.

■ Spinach, currant, asparagus, broccoli, Brussels sprouts: vitamin B-2

■ Kale, parsley, green pepper, and broccoli: vitamin C.

■ Spinach, asparagus, carrot: vitamin E.

■ Red Swiss chard, turnip, garlic, orange: selenium.

■ Carrot, garlic, ginger root: copper.

■ Spinach, turnip greens, beet greens, carrot: manganese.

■ Ginger root, parsley, garlic, carrot: zinc.

These foods and juices will help to keep your eye lenses in good shape. Then they have only heredity to cope with, and there's not much we can do about that.

Besides a good diet, you can go to a rounded intake of vitamins and minerals and supplements especially aimed at helping to prevent cataracts.

## Formula to fight cataracts

Start with a well-rounded multivitamin mineral daily capsule, then supplement it to achieve these levels:

■ Vitamin A—10,000 IU

■ Vitamin C—2,000 mg

■ Vitamin E, as prescribed in your multivitamin mineral supplement

■ Beta-carotene—25,000 IU

■ Zinc—30 mg daily

■ N-acetyl cysteine (NAC)—500 mg (3 times daily)

■ Rutin—250 mg

■ Quercetin—3,000 mg

- Chromium—200 mg
- Riboflavin—50 mg
- Coenzyme Q-10—90 mg
- Curcumin (turmeric). A spice, use liberally. It might come in multivitamin pills.

More and more research I'm seeing shows that vitamin E along with carotenoids and vitamin C may be an effective way to postpone the development of cataracts. Antioxidants such as these interfere with the oxidation of proteins in the eye's lens, which may very well help prevent the lens clouding.

A study at the University of Western Ontario checked vitamin supplements in 175 people with cataracts and 175 without. The patients with cataracts were 44 percent less likely to have consumed vitamin E supplements than their counterparts without cataracts.

Another research study in Finland checked antioxidant blood levels of 47 men and women with cataracts and 94 without cataracts. Low amounts of vitamin E and of beta-carotene were found with an increased risk of developing cataracts. Those having the low figure on vitamin E had a 90 percent higher chance of having cataracts than those with the higher levels of vitamin E.

## Herbal therapy for cataracts

- Use eyebright herb tea as an eyewash.
- Start taking bilberry extract as soon as diagnosed. Helps remove sorbitol accumulation and chemicals from the eyes.
- Take ginkgo biloba extract daily.

- Take Sugar Strategy High capsules for sugar regulation.
- Take high potency royal jelly. Use two teaspoons daily with spirulina tabs. Up to 8 tabs daily.
- Use grapeseed or white pine, 100 mg.
- Try a rose hips eyewash.
- Drink aloe vera juice.

## Homeopathy treatment for cataracts

- Try homeopathic silica or euphrasia tabs.
- Dilute one part cineraria maritime mother tincture in 50 parts spring water. Bathe your eyes in this solution two times a day for three weeks. You may need to contact a homeopathic practitioner in your area to find out where to get this tincture.

# 9 Diabetic Eye Diseases

You probably know someone who has diabetes. Someone you've seen check his or her blood sugar and perhaps use an insulin hypodermic or the new patch. More than 11 million Americans have some form of diabetes.

There are two types of diabetes, and they work differently in the body, but both lead to problems with the eyes. Diabetes is a disease that can adversely affect almost every part of the body. Diabetics have more heart disease, kidney problems, blood vessel disease in the arms and legs, and eye diseases than those people who don't have diabetes.

We're interested in the eyes here. The retina and the eye lens can be affected by diabetes because when the insulin in the body is not effective enough, there is an over-abundance of glucose in the blood. This excess can result in swelling around the macula called macular edema, which can lead to the destruction of vision cells. The body responds by trying to grow new blood cells on the surface of the retina. These weaker blood vessels can break, leading to retinal hemorrhaging into the vitreous gel that makes up the center of the eye.

As with most eye diseases, the patient is rarely aware of any problem when it first begins. For this reason it is mandatory for anyone with diabetes to have an annual visual checkup. Some experts advise a checkup every six months to watch for diabetes-related problems.

One of the first signs of trouble may be small ball-like bulges in the eye's capillaries. As the disease progresses these small balls grow in size and are called "cotton wool spots." The danger here is that they can hemorrhage and leak blood and fluid.

These cotton-wool spots usually mean that some of the retina's cells are dying. This problem doesn't affect the patient's vision, so he or she probably won't go see an ophthalmologist at this point. But, a regularly scheduled six-month exam might catch the problem before it progresses too far.

A drastic change in the patient's diet, with critical nutrients high on the list, can help in this case. If no dietary changes are made, the blood vessels to the macula continue leaking, which makes the nearby retinal tissues swell up. This can leave fatty deposits on the macula. Your doctor can see these as yellowish-white streaks on the macula.

Now the patient will notice a slight blurring of the central vision (reading, fine focus work) and if he hasn't been to see an eye specialist yet, he usually goes now. He has macular edema. If the problem isn't caught at this stage and diagnosed it can lead to severe consequences. The capillaries that feed the retina are severely damaged and in a short time they become useless. This means that part of the eye can't get nourished by the fresh blood supply.

Here the body's recuperative powers take over and try to grow new blood vessels on the surface of the retina to bring in the needed blood. These new vessels are usually weak and soon rupture. This leads to hemorrhaging into the fluid in the center of the eye. Blindness in that eye is a potential danger and usually will occur.

This stage of the development is called diabetic retinopathy.

## Treatments for diabetic retinopathy

The best treatment for any diabetic eye problem is to treat the diabetes first. Get it under control and on an even keel, then look at the specifics.

Exercise has been proven to be one major component that helps diabetics thrive. Work out your own exercise system with a strong emphasis on the aerobic, to keep the blood pumping. Along with that should be a diet that is beneficial for the diabetic situation and good for the eyes. We'll get into this in detail later.

Let's say you go to your ophthalmologist for any number of reasons and he finds that there are the first traces of macular edema. What can he do medically to help you?

First there will be a detailed examination, and then he or she will probably do a fluorescein angiogram. This is a simple process of injecting a harmless dye in a vein in your arm. The blood stream will carry the dye into your eye where the doctor can see clearly if there are any leaks in the blood vessels and exactly where they are.

Now that it has been established that you have diabetic retinopathy, there are two medical procedures that can be used to help.

The first is a laser treatment that is used to cauterize and seal up the leaking blood vessels. This should also slow or stop the swelling called macular edema.

If new blood vessels have grown to supply blood to this area, and some of them are leaking, the procedure is more delicate, since these vessels are younger and weaker than the older ones. This is where blood and fluid can sometimes escape into the inner eye. When this is diagnosed, the doctor can use what is called a scatter laser treatment to stop the bleeding. This isn't a cure-all. Use of the laser at this point is more of a stopgap, but should postpone the loss of vision in this eye for three or four years.

Any surgery on the eye presents dangers. With laser work, reduced peripheral vision and poor dim-light vision can be serious side effects. That's why you'll want to talk over any eye surgery carefully with your doctor, perhaps get a second opinion, and be sure that surgery is best for your near—and long-term eyesight.

If your eye has developed hemorrhages that leak blood and fluid into the vitreous humor of the middle of the eye, a different procedure is called for. This is a vitrectomy. Here the doctor uses delicate and precision instruments to pull the blood and fluids out of the vitreous humor.

When successful, this opens up the eye again for clear passage of the light coming through the lens and aimed at the retina.

## Good nutrition extremely important

If diabetics want to live very long, they know they must pay special attention to their diet and their lifestyle. That's the regimen.

Diabetics must first of all control the blood sugar level in their bodies. Without this control nothing else matters. By necessity, diabetics learn to test their blood sugar level three or four times a day to control their systems.

Most adults with type II diabetes can keep from using insulin and diabetes drugs if they change their lifestyle sufficiently. This means a closely controlled diet and exercise. The exercise should come at least five times a week, a half-hour at a time. Aerobic exercises are simplest and often the most productive. We covered these in detail in chapter 7. The same rules and plans apply here as well.

Diet is another feat. The two big changes are to attempt to eliminate sugar and refined grains from any of the food you eat. This means no white bread or cakes or cookies or pasta made from refined flour. Even chips and white rice must be cut out.

In their place look for whole grain breads and rolls. There are many more of them on the market now, and they are delicious. Even some whole grain bagels are showing up.

Many experts now say that sugar substitutes are not a good thing for diabetics, especially NutraSweet. The chemical name for this is aspartame, and it's simply not good for diabetics and anyone with eye problems. It is a known eye toxin and has a number of side effects hazardous to those already experiencing vision problems.

Often the sweetest food you can eat is without refined sugar. It comes in the form of fruits and dates and honey. Some say that the most delicious and sweetest of all the fruits is the pear. Give a ripe pear a try.

A good diet for maintaining your blood sugar at a stable level is to stick with these old reliables: lots of vegetables of all types, colors, and varieties. Load up on eggs, meat, fish, chicken, turkey and tofu, brown rice, and whole grain breads. Don't forget the fruit side (for the bioflavonoids) such as blueberries, red onions, raspberries, and cherries.

## What about vitamins and supplements?

Experience shows that changing a diet for a diabetic will change the blood sugar level as well. This might make it go up or down depending on the type of food eaten.

So, using this vitamin and supplement regimen will also change the diabetic's blood sugar level. Usually this will bring it down, so do your tests four times a day and stand by for more good things to happen.

- First a good high-potency complete multivitamin and mineral supplement
- Vitamin B: usually your multivitamin capsule is enough
- Vitamin C: 2,000 mg (more if you're ill)
- Vitamin E: your multivitamin has enough
- Beta-carotene: your multivitamin is enough
- Chromium: 200 mcg
- Quercetin: 1,000 mg
- Vanadyl sulfate: 20 mg
- Magnesium: 400 mg (at bedtime)
- N-acetyl cysteine: 500 mg, 3 times between meals
- Garlic: 1 raw clove, or 1,000 mg capsule
- Omega-3 oils: from cold water fish, 3 times weekly
- L-carnitine: 500 mg
- Zinc: enough in your multivitamins

# 10 Retinitis Pigmentosa

CHAPTER

Retinitis pigmentosa is one of the worst kinds of eye diseases. It actually includes 14 different kinds of eye disorders involving the retina's surface/pigmented cells.

The mechanics work this way. The visual pigments are part of the retina that makes the eyes' sensitivity to light possible. They undergo a constant rotation as older cells are shed off, and they are replaced with new pigment cells.

Problems occur when the worn out pigment cells clump together on the retina, and the normal process of washing them away does not work.

A small percentage of people with eye diseases have retinitis pigmentosa (RP).

The first symptoms often show up in childhood, and the majority of cases are genetically linked. The first sign may be night blindness. There may be a loss of side vision that is progressive and happens to people in their 30s. Tunnel vision develops during the patient's 40s with total blindness soon thereafter.

At this time there is no known medical treatment for this disease at any of the stages.

We mentioned before that the retinal transplant experiments are now going on, which may have some value, but any actual use of such a treatment is many years away.

RP is not the only problem for these patients. As many as 50 percent of RP patients will also develop cataracts, and nearly all will have problems reading, adjusting to bright lights, and focusing. Since the eventual outcome of the disease is well known, most patients also suffer from depression, anger, anxiety, and headaches.

Anyone who has been diagnosed with RP must realize that the immediate situation is not hopeless. We are going to show you good eye practices that may very well slow down the development of RP and lead to many more years of at least marginal sight.

The key here, as with most retinal problems, is the oxidation of cells. We'll have more to say later about the practice of working toward the best possible antioxidant benefits for your eyes. One of the secrets here is boosting your glutathione levels.

This is one of the several antioxidants that your body makes. It is a part of every living cell in our bodies. Healthy people manufacture as much as 14,000 mg of glutathione a day. This is moved through the bloodstream to every cell in your body.

The body needs sulfur to make it, so foods rich in sulfur are important. These include eggs, garlic, onions, and asparagus. You can get a biological sulfur supplement—MSM Powder—at health food stores.

Glutathione itself is not stable outside the body, so the best way to increase it is to take into your system some of its building blocks. One is the amino acid cysteine. We've mentioned this before in supplement lists. It's in the form of N-acetyl cysteine/NAC. Another supplement to help is alpha lipoic acid.

Vitamins C and E, selenium, and beta-carotene help glutathione do its work.

While about half of all people with RP have a family history of the disease, the other half don't. Here are a few things you can do to decrease your chances of getting RP if you are in the nonhereditary group.

- Avoid long exposure to intense sunlight. Those ultraviolet and blue-violet sun rays can harm the night vision elements in your eyes, cutting down on your night vision.

- Avoid a diet high in unsaturated or hydrogenated oils. These can come from corn and safflower oil and are often found in margarine.

- Avoid a diet low in essential fatty acids such as found in fresh vegetables. These are omega-3 and omega-6, which are essential for good night vision.

- Avoid drugs such as Mellaril, tetracycline, diuretics, sulfas, and thiazide tranquilizers These are photosensitizing drugs and bad for your eyes.

## What about a cure?

Retinitis pigmentosa is a series of conditions of the retina and not a disease as such. At the present time there are no medical treatments, surgeries, or drugs to stop or reverse this condition. If the RP includes cataracts, they can be removed with good results, but that doesn't eliminate the RP.

Scatter laser treatments can sometimes bring down the swelling of the macula and seal off new blood vessels. These are spot aids and are again not a cure for RP.

Experimental work is now underway with hyperbaric oxygen, in which the RP patient inhales pressurized oxygen. Some studies show that will slow the progression of RP. This is still experimental and tremendously expensive.

## Can you slow RP's progression?

Yes, more and more people, including doctors and nutritionists, say they think there is a link between the foods we eat, the supplements we take, and the progress of RP. It hasn't been proven scientifically yet, but there are enough indicators and proponents that I think it's worth trying.

Look at it this way. If two or three people in your family have RP, your doctor will probably say the chances of you getting it are high.

Why not try to fight it off for as long as possible with the use of good nutrition and supplements? For those who don't have a family history of RP, these supplements and good nutrition aimed at helping the eyes might just be the ticket to helping you remain RP free. Either way, it's a good chance that the best eye nutrition and supplements aimed at helping your eyes can go a long way toward postponing or avoiding RP.

The beauty of it is that it's the type of program that in no way can hurt you. Any help to your body from better nutrition and the use of supplements helps your whole system, not just your eyes. There is absolutely no way that you can lose.

It's the money argument, too. Say there was a medical operation that might help your RP. You'd grab it even if it cost $820,000. So what's the big deal about spending a relatively small amount of money on vitamins and supplements each month?

Try these ideas for your first assault in your new aggressive attack on RP:

- Keep a chart to record your 30-minute walk every day.

- Make sure your multivitamin does not contain iron.

- Be sure not to use any unsaturated oils in cooking or in margarine spreads.

- Make sure you get enough omega-3 and -6 fatty acids. One good way is to eat salmon, cod, or sardines three times a week.

- Be sure you don't get overstressed. Talk to friends; obtain professional help if you need it.

- Eat both lutein-rich food and beta-carotene-rich food. Try to alternate them so they will enhance absorption and provide the most benefits.

- Tell your doctor you can't take drugs that put any undue stress on your liver. Also throw away all of your Tylenol. It is a high liver-stress agent.

- Try never to use photosensitizing drugs. There are dozens of these including diuretics, Tylenol and Advil, most antibiotics, and sulfas.

- Keep away from eye toxins such as monosodium glutamate (MSG) and NutraSweet (aspartame).

- Cut down on refined sugars and refined carbohydrates.

- Wear those sunglasses that "wrap around" to protect your eyes from ultraviolet rays.

- Don't smoke; stay away from people who do.

- Stop drinking alcohol. You need your liver in tip-top shape to make loads of glutathione and to pump vitamin A to your eyes.

## What supplements can help your RP?

- Beta-carotene, B vitamins, zinc, and vitamin E as included in daily multivitamins

- Vitamin C: 2,000 mg

- Bioflavonoids: 400 mg

- Quercetin: 1,500 mg

- Coenzyme Q-10: 200 mg

- Cayenne pepper capsules: 2 capsules with meals.

- Ginkgo biloba: 360 mg

- Lutein/zeaxanthin: 12 mg. Take separately from beta-carotene.

- N-acetyl cysteine (NAC): 500 mg Three times a day between meals.

- Bilberry and grapeseed: As shown on package.

- Magnesium: 400 mg

- Alpha lipoic acid: 300 mg

- Taurine: 1,000 mg

- L-Carnitine: 1,500 mg

# 11 Glaucoma

The most feared and least understood of all the eye diseases is glaucoma. This disease is the one that causes more people in the United States to go blind than any other.

Some call it the silent thief of your eyesight, since it can strike suddenly after developing for years without you knowing it and shut off the sight of one or both eyes.

Many experts now say what we call glaucoma is probably the end product of a number of systemic diseases and structural faults that create high pressure inside the eye and damage the optic nerve. Such pressure can damage and even kill the highly sensitive nerve cells on the retina resulting in the loss of sight.

The problem has been around a long time. The ancient Greeks named the disease, and we still don't know enough about it today.

Most eye specialists diagnose glaucoma by three factors. First the intraocular pressure, usually called IOP. That's the pressure inside the eye which usually is higher than normal with glaucoma. Then they look for specific changes in the patient's visual field. Often this is the loss of peripheral vision. Then the last point to check is to see if there are any signs of damage to the optic nerve itself.

Most eye checks during physicals these days, and when being tested for new glasses, include a routine check for glaucoma. This is often a "puff of air" test, but it is indicative. This can show an increase in the IOP, the pressure inside the eye. This method is how most glaucoma is found, and often in its early stages when it can be treated better. Whenever you have an eye exam, ask for a glaucoma test as well.

Why does pressure build up in your eye?

The eye is filled with fluid and there is a constant supply of new fluid. This means some of the older fluid must drain off to maintain the proper level and at the correct pressure.

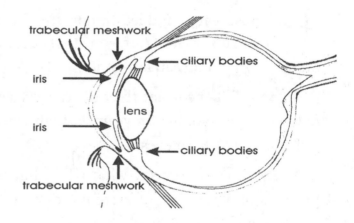

The problem comes when there is a stoppage or a slow down in draining the fluid out. There is a build up and this increased pressure can result in the death of the optic nerve cells. They are destroyed from the outside side edge of the retina toward the center. One of the advanced symptoms of glaucoma is tunnel vision.

When the eye is working properly, the excess fluid secreted by the ciliary body works out through a tiny opening between the lens and the iris of your eye to enter what's called an anterior chamber. Then it drains out through the trabecular meshwork.

There are more than a dozen types of glaucoma. We'll look at the most common.

## Open angle glaucoma

In this type there is a blockage of the fluid escaping from the eye, but it is a partial stoppage and not completely blocked. This increases the pressure within the eye. You are more susceptible to this type of glaucoma if you smoke or drink too much, are African American, or have clogged arteries, diabetes, high blood pressure, or a history of severe anemia.

Many experts believe that about 85 percent of all glaucoma cases are of this type.

This one may be the worst, since there are no symptoms, no pain, and it can progress slowly over the years. By the time the victim notices it, or it is diagnosed, a lot of vision has already been destroyed.

## Closed angle glaucoma

In this type the tiny drainage canals within the eye that regulate the supply of fluid and pressure within the eyeball are completely blocked. This can be for a number of different reasons. It can be mechanical: the shape of the eye lends itself to this problem. Perhaps the lens of the eye bulges too far forward. Sometimes the iris pigment layer thickens, and this can close the drain tube. In some cases the iris actually moves forward and touches the cornea, closing off the only drainage area.

## Secondary glaucomas

When glaucoma is caused by a disease, it is called a secondary glaucoma. There is nothing cut and dried here. Sometimes a disease will cause glaucoma in one person but the same ailment will not cause that problem in another person. Sometimes there is more than one problem that causes glaucoma to develop in an individual.

Over the years of careful research and case histories, certain conclusions have been made about several of these secondary glaucomas. Here they are:

❶ **Exfoliation syndrome:** this is caused when cells inside the eye flake off. These cells may be from the epithelial or lining cells, in the front, of the eye. Under a microscope they look like dandruff. These small flakes settle in the trabecular meshwork. Usually this is the escape area for fluid to leave the eye. If the flakes clog up this meshwork, the fluid can't drain away, so fluid and pressure buildup quickly follow.

Exfoliation is a tough one to diagnose, and often it progresses and can eventually lead to blindness. Once the problem is discovered the treatment is much the same as used with open angle glaucoma: medication in eye drops, laser treatment, and then surgery.

❷ **Uveitis:** this general term describes an inflammation inside the eye. The uvea is the middle layer in the material covering your eyes: the one that has the blood vessels, the ciliary body, and the iris. The ending letters, "itis," simply mean inflammation.

At first doctors thought this was caused by some kind of virus. The trouble is, in many cases of uveitis there is no virus to be found.

More recent work in this area is developing the idea that the problem may be one of an autoimmune nature. In this situation the immune system in the body for some reason attacks the body's own tissue.

This means there may be some antigen that provokes the formation of antibodies in the retina. Discovering how to deal with that kind of an antigen in the retina is a huge problem.

Not everyone who has uveitis will develop glaucoma, and no one knows why. When a person with uveitis does develop glaucoma, it usually is due to inflammation of both the ciliary body and the trabecular meshwork.

Just how uveitis develops into glaucoma is not known. Some say that the inflammation itself leads to glaucoma. When inflamed, the ciliary body slows down in the production of the aqueous fluid. This can cause structural changes in the eye.

Inflammation anywhere in the body is a clarion call for the white blood cells to rush in and kill off the bad guys. Happens in the eye too. Too many of these white blood cells and the damage from the inflammation can sometimes overwork the trabecular network. Then, the cells can't reproduce themselves as fast as usual, and the whole system starts to break down. The meshwork gets clogged, and the fluid is blocked from leaving the eye through the normal drainage system. The pressure inside the eye increases, and we have glaucoma.

Anytime an eye specialist tells you that you have uveitis, be sure to ask him to check as well for glaucoma. If you do have it, you probably found it early. Many doctors say that with early treatment, glaucoma can be controlled.

❸ **Normal tension glaucoma:** this is a strange one and goes against the grain of the others. Here the optic nerve begins to die, even though the pressure within the eye is in the normal pressure range of 10 to 21 Hg.

No one knows why. There are a lot of theories: hemorrhages of the optic nerve disc, a misshapen optic nerve head, a diminished blood supply to the optic nerve, low blood pressure, myopia, high blood pressure, vascular disease, carotid artery disease, and migraines.

Some doctors say someone with this problem should have a complete physical examination by a medical doctor familiar with cardiovascular and neurological disorders. It should include complete blood count, serum chemistries, carotid blood evaluation, erythrocyte sedimentation rate, and even a CT scan. Pressure in the eye is still thought to be the culprit by many ophthalmologists who say reducing the pressure even further to 8 to 12 Hg may be helpful.

❹ **Neovascular glaucomas:** the first word simply means new blood vessels, and that is what happens in a number of different diseases that affect the orderly flow of blood to and from the retina. Three of these types will be discussed below.

They all happen when the fine balance between the stimulation and inhibition of the carotid arteries and the central retinal vein becomes upset. The arteries bring blood to the head, and the veins return it to the heart. Blockage of this blood supply is the problem. When that happens, in all three of these diseases, the regular blood vessels in the retina are starved for oxygen from the blood.

The body tries to compensate by releasing substances that grow new blood vessels. They often grow wildly over the retina, the optic nerve, the iris, and the trabecular network. They are fragile and easily ruptured, and really mess up your eyesight.

Let's look at each of the three:

*Diabetic retinopathy:* this problem can affect 50 percent of diabetics. The situation here is that errant blood vessels travel to places they don't belong—grow over the iris, the drainage channels, and the retina and can damage nerve tissue and clog up eye drainage.

When this happens your doctor can prescribe medications to help curb this excess of the retinal vein. A laser treatment may be suggested. If the diabetic can keep his blood sugar under control, it may be possible for him or her to avoid this disease entirely.

Looking ahead—researchers are working on transplanting insulin-producing pancreatic cells into the retina to help with minute-to-minute blood sugar control.

Another hope is a drug called pentoxifylline that should be nearly out of clinical trials. Hopefully, it will slow the progression of early diabetic retinopathy.

*Central retinal vein occlusion:* as the name implies, in this disease the central vein in the retina sending blood back to the heart becomes blocked. Who gets this disease most? Those with diabetes, high blood pressure, polycythemia, or any other condition that affects blood flow. This is usually a disease associated with people over 60 years of age.

When the return of blood from the retina is blocked, this affects the incoming blood, and the retina is starved for fresh oxygen in the blood. This results in neovascular glaucoma.

Some experts call this the 100-day glaucoma, since there are no immediate symptoms when the blockage takes place.

Even so, doctors say that 80 percent of those with this type of blockage will develop glaucoma within six months.

*Carotid artery occlusive disease:* this one is caused by the hardening of the carotid artery, one on either side of the neck, that takes, blood to the head, brain, and retina.

When these arteries become narrowed there can be an effect on the retina. Severe cases can lead to blindness. The retinal cells can die if there is a greatly reduced supply of blood and the oxygen it brings.

A severe case of hardening of the carotid arteries would also put your brain in a great deal of trouble.

## How can glaucoma be treated?

❶ Drugs are the most common treatment. These drugs are designed to lower the fluid pressure around the optic nerve. If you have ocular hypertension or primary open angle glaucoma, your eye specialist may prescribe one of these drugs:

### Epinephrine/sympathomimetic eye drops

Most medications for glaucoma are eye drops. They get directly to the problem area and do their work.

This steps up the flow of the fluid draining from your eyes. In some people the drops will cause burning and stinging, and vision may be blurry for a while. But that will pass.

If you have any history of diabetes, overactive thyroid gland, high blood pressure, heart disease, asthma, or stroke, these eye drops should be used with critical caution. For these at-risk patients, the drops can cause an increase in blood pressure, cause the heart to race, and can cause angina pains. Some patients feel faint or light-headed when using this medication.

Many ophthalmologists do not recommend these drops because of the dangers to so many patients. They say there are other drugs that are just as reliable and do the job without the dangerous side effects.

One of those is Dipivefrin HCL. This drop turns into epinephrine when put into the eye. Even so, the side effects are much milder and there is much less stinging. Some patients with heart problems and high blood pressure may still have problems, but they are not as severe as with the other drug.

## Beta blocker eye drops

There are a number of name brands of these beta blocker eye drops. Their job is to decrease the pressure in the eye by slowing the production of the fluid. They work. They also have a lot of side effects. Some people experience decreased sex drive, depression, lowered heart rate, breathing problems, and even a loss of balance.

If you have asthma, forget the beta blockers. If you take beta blockers for some other ailment, do not double up and take them for glaucoma as well. Perhaps you can reduce or eliminate the beta blockers for the other problem, then use them to fight the glaucoma.

A warning here. Use only the dose of beta blockers that is prescribed by your eye specialist. Too much of this medication can have seriously bad results.

## Miotics/parasympathomimetic eye drops

These drops are usually composed of pilocarpine or carbachol or various combinations of the two. Here you will find more than a dozen brand names with these ingredients. They all do a good job to increase the drainage of fluids from the eye.

A good feature here is that these have fewer side effects than the other eye pressure relief drugs we've been talking about. They work by changing the dimensions of the lens by stimulating the muscles that do this job. The smaller lens increases the drainage.

Those with secondary glaucoma usually can't use these drugs. Patients with cramps in the digestive tract, urinary tract obstructions, ulcers, hyperthyroidism, Parkinson's disease, recent heart attacks, or either low or high blood pressure are advised as well not to take this eye drop medication.

Problems from the use of these miotics include causing the retina to become detached. Be sure to have your doctor double check your condition before you take any miotic medication. Also you'll want to be careful when driving at night or in any dim light because the drops will affect your ability to function in dark environments.

Any of these miotic medications will sting when the drops are put in the eyes. They also might cause headaches. Don't take these drops if you have asthma either.

## Prostaglandin eye drops

These drops of Xalatan increase the drainage of aqueous humor and decrease the pressure of the fluid inside the eye. The drops have fewer side effects than the beta blockers. An interesting side effect though is that the color of your eyes may change from blue or green to brown when this medication is used.

You also may have temporary blurred vision and some burning when using these drops.

Even so, most eye specialists consider these comparatively new drops as the best for treating glaucoma.

❷ Surgery can be a glaucoma treatment. As with other types of eye problems, surgery is the last resort treatment for patients with glaucoma. If other methods don't stop the damage to the optic nerve, then surgery is the only option left.

More and more eye specialists are recommending now that an aggressive program of nutritional treatment be instigated at the first sign of eye trouble, especially with glaucoma. Good nutrition, aimed specifically at helping the eye to adjust and weather the disease, may be an important factor in clearing up some of these eye problems. We talk more about this in the next few pages.

A lifestyle change can also help, even if it's only the use of a good pair of eye-protective sunglasses every time you are in the sun or under bright lights.

When you are diagnosed with some type of eye disease or problem, you must insist on having a frank and thorough discussion with your doctor about your eyes. For example, is your hand steady enough to put drops in your eyes on a consistent basis? Is your memory sharp enough for you to remember to use the eye drops when they must be taken?

## Laser surgery

As we said, eye surgery is usually the last hope. One type is laser surgery, the trabeculoplasty. The purpose is to help drain the excess fluid out of your eye and reduce the eye pressure. In most cases you will still need to take your glaucoma drugs after the surgery.

Laser surgery works this way:

It is an outpatient procedure done in a clinic or an eye specialist's office. First he or she will apply drops to numb your eye.

You'll sit facing the laser machine much like the testing one you were at before. The doctor will hold a special lens to your eye. A high-energy beam of light is aimed at the lens and reflected into the meshwork, where your eye fluid is supposed to drain. Flashes of bright red or green light may be seen.

The laser is quickly burning 50 to 100 evenly spaced spots on your meshwork. These burns stretch the drainage holes in the meshwork. Now the fluid should drain out of them and reduce your eye pressure to normal.

The doctor will check your eye pressure shortly after the surgery. You may have drops to use in case of any soreness or swelling inside the eye. You'll make several follow up calls to your doctor for evaluation.

When laser surgery works to reduce the pressure, it usually is good for only about two years, and then the pressure builds back up. The laser surgery can be repeated.

## Conventional surgery

The other kind of surgery on the eye is called a trabeculectomy. This procedure makes a new opening for the excess fluid to leave the eye, bypassing the clogged up meshwork. The surgery is usually not done unless medicine and laser surgery do not lower the eye pressure.

Now we are in an eye clinic or a hospital for this surgery. For this, a pressure-relief valve is surgically made from the eye's natural tissues. It's done by removing a small piece of tissue from the white of the eye. This creates a new channel for the fluid to drain away from the eye.

The "hole" in the eye is then covered by the conjunctiva, a clear tissue that covers the white of the eye. This protects the eye and leaves the canal open for the fluid to drain out.

Drops will be needed in your eye for several weeks after the operation to control any infection or swelling. You'll also need to make several visits to your doctor for eye examinations. In the general population, this type of surgery is as much as 90 percent effective in lowering the pressure. There's a chance the opening may grow shut. If so, another operation can be done. These surgeries will not improve your sight, but they may mean it will not get any worse. You're looking at the long-term here.

If it works, it usually is good for about five years before the operation is needed again. But, another operation could mean five more years of eyesight for you.

Another procedure involves inserting a synthetic drain into the eye where the blockage takes place. This is sometimes used when the eye does not respond to the eye drops or other surgical treatments.

❸ Good nutrition and supplements can be used as treatments. By eating right, you can also be treating your glaucoma. A balanced diet with a strong surge of fresh vegetables and fruit and three servings of cold water fish a week can help keep your eyes in better condition and perhaps have a big part in curing the problem.

Concentrate on proteins with a low-fat content such as turkey, chicken, eggs, and soy products such as tofu. The more vegetables you eat, the more vitamins A, D, and B you need. Be sure you are getting enough.

The cause of your eye problem could have been accelerated because the blood flow to your retina was not sufficient. These good foods will help increase the blood flow to your retina and could help slow your disease.

Other foods that are "good health" for your eyes include: spinach, almonds, onions, olive oil for cooking, eggs, asparagus, carrots, cold water fish, cantaloupe, watermelon, and avocados.

While not actually nutrition, here's something to go easy on. Coffee. Caffeine in particular. That third cup of coffee for the day may be harming your vision. Research experts at the University of Texas and at Emory University say that caffeine can increase the pressure in your eyes, which is the major factor in glaucoma. Caffeine comes in many drinks but primarily coffee, tea, and cola drinks. Two cups a day is enough, but why not just cut out all caffeine?

It will be better for your eyes. Yes, you may have a headache the second or third day of "cold turkey," but that will pass quickly, and then you're off caffeine and onto better eye health.

## Vitamins and food supplements to fight glaucoma:

- Vitamin A: 10,000 IU
- Vitamin B complex: as in your multivitamins
- Vitamin C: 1,000 mg
- Carnitine: 500 mg
- Carotenoids: a mixture supplement includes 25,000 IU beta-carotene, 1 mg of alpha-carotene, 5 mg of lycopene, 6 mg of lutein, and 0.3 mg of zeaxanthin. Use this between meals or at a meal where you do not eat a lot of beta-carotene-rich foods.
- Chromium: 200-600 mg if you are using beta blocker eye drops
- Coenzyme Q-10:200 mg. Take with ginger root if you have a low-pressure glaucoma.
- Coleus: 400 mg. This is a centuries old herbal medicine to relax muscles in blood vessel walls, easing high blood pressure and ocular hypertension. Sold under the name of Forskohlii.
- Vitamin E: as indicated on your multivitamin
- Garlic: 1 raw clove with food or 1,000 mg capsule
- Omega-3 fish oil: 1,000 mg
- Magnesium: 400 mg at bedtime
- Quercetin: 1,000-3,000 mg
- Rutin: 3,000 mg
- Zinc: as contained in your multivitamin

# 12 Bits and Pieces

CHAPTER

Here are some small items that didn't fit in too well in the previous chapters, but that I wanted to bring to your attention.

## A nice treat

Want to give your eyes a break? Try palming them. All you do is close your eyes and cover them with the palms of your hands. Then luxuriate in the total blackness. Don't touch your eyes with your palms. If you're working your eyes hard, do this for two or three minutes every two hours and you'll notice the difference.

## Sunshade tips

When you buy sunglasses, make sure they do the right job as well as look right.

- Put on your chosen sunglasses and look in a mirror. In ordinary room light you should just be able to see your own eyes. That's about the right density for driving and outdoor work.

■ Look through the glasses at the edge of a doorway. Concentrate on the straight vertical line. Move your head from side to side. If the straight line wiggles, there is some imperfection in the lens. Try on another pair.

■ Check green and red objects in the room or the mall. Can you pick out the green ones from the reds through your new shades? Gray and brown lenses give you the truest color vision. Ask how much UV-A and UV-B radiation the lenses block. They should be 100 percent on both. Also ask about blue ultraviolet light blockage. It should be 75 percent. If the clerk doesn't know, have him find out, or go to another store. He may have to phone the manufacturer.

## The old eyebath

Pour lukewarm water into a bowl. Dissolve a teaspoon of salt in the water. Put your face in the water covering your eyes. Now open your eyes. Stay underwater for 30 seconds. Come out and take some deep breaths, then have another 30-second open eye bath. A good way to totally relax your eyes. The salt bath can't hurt either.

## Take care of your eyes

■ Give your eyes a break every 20 minutes during hard work times. Look out a window to the farthest point you can see. Change your focus for three minutes.

■ Try this. Slant your desk upward at a 20-degree angle. When you look at your work now it will be at a 90-degree angle to your line of sight, instead of 110 degrees or more. It makes focusing on the material easier. You can do the same thing with an empty, two-inch, three-ring binder. Lay it with the large section away from you. Place your study work on the slant toward you. Easier reading, easier on your eyes.

## Yoga might help

Yoga can strengthen your eye muscles and improve your vision with a series of simple yoga exercises. Sitting in a straight backed chair:

- With your left hand in your lap, stretch your right arm straight out in front of you at eye level with your palm facing you. Make a gentle fist and raise your index finger. With both eyes, look down your nose. Then focus on your index finger. Then look as far into the distance as you can. Then look back at your nose. Do this five times. Repeat the exercise with your right hand in your lap. There is a reason for the arm extension: your eyes take turns "dominating" depending on which arm is extended.

- Sit with your hands in your lap. Keep your head straight up and look forward. Without moving your head, look to the right with both eyes, then straight ahead, then left, and again straight ahead. Repeat this five times.

- Close your eyes tightly, then open them wide looking at an object far off in the distance. Do this 10 times.

APPENDIX

# Exercises For Your Whole Body

While your aerobic exercises are good for you, your eyes, and blood circulation, they can be only the first step in a whole body exercise program.

Here are a series of exercises that are gentle on the body and won't cause you any pain. They are designed to help you get in a half-hour more of a workout either after or before your aerobic work.

Take these one at a time. Do maybe two or three the first day, and keep at those for a week. The second week you may want to add two or three more.

Don't do any of them if they give you a hurt back or pains in your joints. These exercises are not the "no pain, no gain" type. They are put together to help you feel good, have a better physical body, and enrich your health and your life.

Now, get out there and do some exercising!

## Exercises For Your Whole Body

### #1  One Arm, One Leg Raise

■ Lie on a pad with your
right arm extended
over your head. Rest
your head on your arm. Left arm straight, hand at waist.

■ Lift your left leg to a 45-degree or greater angle.

■ Now raise your left arm to a 45-degree or greater angle and at
the same time return your left leg to the start position.

■ Return your left arm to original position and at the same
time, raise your left leg again.

■ Repeat number of reps desired, then turn and do the same
number on your other side.

### #2  Side Stretch Lifts

■ Lie on your right side
with arms in front at
your waist. Have some-
one hold down your
feet, or put them under
the edge of a piece of
heavy furniture.

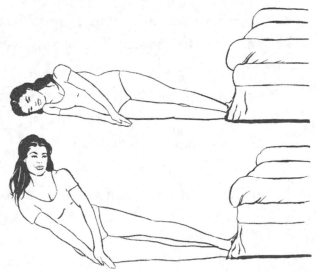

■ Lift your body from
the waist up several
inches and strain for
a few seconds.

- Lower to starting position. Do desired number of reps.
- Turn over and repeat sequence on your left side.

## #3 Curl-up Twist

- Lie on your back with knees bent and hands crossed on your chest or behind your neck.
- Curl your head and shoulders off the floor by tightening your abdominal muscles. Keep your back on the floor.
- As you come upward twist to the right and hold for six seconds.
- Return to starting position.
- Repeat curl-up and twist to your left.
- Return to starting position.
- Do desired number of reps.

## #4 One Leg Side Raise

- Lie on your right side, head resting on extended right arm. Left hand on floor at your waist for support.
- Lift your left leg to at 45-degree or more angle.

- Return leg to start position.
- Repeat number of reps.
- Turn over and do on the other side desired number of reps.

## #5 Double Knee Swings

- Lie on your back, arms extended, knees drawn up to chest.

- Keep knees together and swing them to the right until knee touches the floor.
- Return to start position, pause.
- Swing knees to the left until knee touches the floor.
- Return to start position.
- Do desired number of reps.

## #6 Shoulder Crunch

- Lie on the floor, legs bent at a 45-degree angle, hands behind head.
- Flexing abdominals, raise head and shoulders off the floor as far as possible.
- Do not lift back off floor.

- Straining, hold position for six seconds.
- Gently lower shoulders and head to floor.
- Repeat desired number of reps.

## #7 Sitting "V"

- Sit on the floor with your legs extended, hands beside your hips on the floor.
- Lift your legs off the floor, keepin body backward until you form a "V." Your back should be slightly rounded.
- Hold the "V" for six seconds.
- Slowly return to start position.
- Repeat desired number of reps.

## #8 Bent Knee Leg Lift

- Lie on back with legs straight out on the floor and arms at your sides.
- Bring both knees hard against your chest, keeping back flat against the floor.
- Lift both legs upward with knees straight so your body forms an "L.'

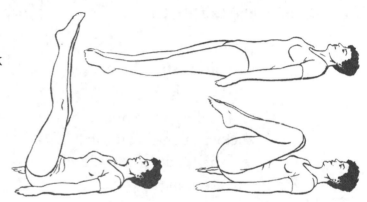

- Return your knees to your chest.
- Return legs flat to the floor.
- Repeat number of desired reps.

So, there you have your workout for the day. But you're not done once you finish your reps for exercise #8. Now comes your cool down process.

If you quit exercising cold turkey, you can create problems. Your body has been revved up to some serious exercise, now suddenly you stop, and it doesn't know what to do. You need to cool down gradually, to let your muscles relax and not work so hard. Your heartbeat needs to come down slowly to your normal level. Your respiration also will slow down a little at a time.

A sudden stop of exercises after strenuous exercise can cause blood to collect in muscle tissue and veins which can lead to weakness and a sudden dizziness and black spots in front of your eyes.

So, take a few minutes and do these cool down exercises after each workout session.

## Cool Down Exercises

### Achilles and Calf Stretch

- Stand near a wall. Lean out with arms straight, hands on the wall.
- Gradually work your feet backward until you can feel the tendons stretching and straining in the back of your leg and ankle.

■ Keep your feet flat on the floor. Stretch the tendons slightly more by bending your arms a little and leaning farther forward. Hold this stretching for 20 seconds. Then relax.

## Light Back Stretch

■ Sit flat on the floor with legs in front.

■ Allow your right leg to stay straight, place your left foot on the floor on the other side of your right knee.

■ Hold your straight leg with your right hand. Left hand on your hip.

■ Twist upper body to the left as far as possible. Tighten muscles and hold for six seconds.

■ Return to start position.

■ Repeat with other leg, reversing legs, hands and twist.

■ Do this exercise three times.

## High Stretch

■ Stand with feet apart, keep legs straight.

■ Place right hand on your right hip, fully extend your left hand over your head.

- Bend slowly to the right. Hold the position for six seconds.
- Change arm positions and bend to the other side and hold for six seconds.
- Repeat this exercise three times.

## Alternate Exercises

### #9  Double Leg Side Lift

- Lie on your right side, one arm stretched out with your head resting on it. Legs together. Left hand palm down on floor beside your chest.
- Keep legs together and lift them six inches to a foot off the floor. Hold for three seconds.
- Slowly lower legs to start position.
- Repeat doing desired number of reps.
- Turn on other side and repeat the exercise doing desired number of reps.

### #10  Lay Down Foot To Finger

- Lie on your back with your legs together. Push out your arms fully on each side on the floor.

- Lift right leg to vertical.

- Keep knee from bending and swing right leg to the floor to touch your left fingers.

- Return leg to vertical, then lower to floor to start position.

- Do the same exercise with your left leg.

- Repeat for the desired number of reps.

## #11 Rise Up and Twist

- Lie flat on the floor on your back, bend your knees upward, lock fingers behind your head.

- Gently curl up into a sitting position. First draw your chin toward your chest, then lift your torso upward with stomach muscles. Back should be gently rounded.

- Twist your upper body and touch your right elbow to your right knee.

- Return to starting position.

- Repeat exercise touching left elbow to left knee.

- Do the desired number of reps. (Notice: If this exercise hurts your back, do not use it.)

## #12 Slide Up and Twist

- Lie flat on the floor, legs together, arms stretched down middle of your body.

■ Lift your upper body off the floor as a sit up, and at the same time bend up your knees and slide your feet toward your buttocks. Stop at a 45-degree angle. Keep back straight.

■ As you curl upward, turn your upper body to the left and touch both hands to the floor on your left.

■ Return to starting position.

■ Repeat desired number of reps alternating sides with the twist. (Notice: If this exercise hurts your back, don't use it.)

## #13 Let Down Crunch

■ Sit on the floor and bend your knees up to a 45-degree angle and your hands behind your head.

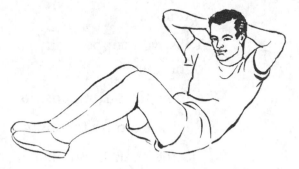

■ Lower slowly your torso backwards to a 45-degree angle. You'll feel your muscles begin to pull.

■ Hold for four seconds, then slowly return to start position.

■ Repeat the exercise for the desired reps.

## #14  Bent Leg Sit-Ups

- Lie on your back, legs bent at 45-degree angle, arms lax at your sides.

- Pull down chin toward your chest then lift your torso up in classic sit-up. Back should be slightly rounded.

- Return to start position.

- Repeat exercise the desired number of reps. (Notice: If this exercise hurts your back, don't use it.)

## #15  Bent Knee Single Leg Lift

- Lie on your back, left leg bent upward at 45 degrees. Right leg flat on floor. Hands on your hips.

- Lift your right leg straight up to vertical. Keep the small of your back firmly against the floor.

- Bring down your right leg to the floor.

- Repeat desired number of reps.

- Now reverse legs and do the exercise the desired number of reps lifting your left leg.

## #16 Floor Bicycling

- Sit on the pad with your hands by your hips and your legs extended.

- Lift one leg up and pull toward your chest. Lean back a little and keep your back slightly rounded.

- Lift your other leg off the floor and simulate a bicycle motion with both legs but don't touch the floor.

- Each stroke with your left leg is one rep. Do three times the desired reps.

## #17 Curl Toe Touches

- Lie on floor with legs stretched out fully and arms near your sides.

- Curl your body forward in near sit up position and at the same time lift your left leg and lift right arm and touch your left toes.

- Return to start position.

- Curl up again using other hand to touch your other toe and return to start position.

- Repeat desired number of reps. (Notice: If this exercise hurts your back, don't use it.)

## #18  V Seat Walking

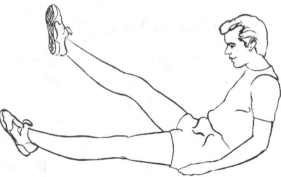

■ Sit on floor with legs extended and your hands on the floor near your hips.

■ Lift your legs off the floor to a 45-degree angle and lean torso slightly to the rear for balance. Back is slightly rounded.

■ Move your legs up and down in opposite directions as if walking without touching the floor.

■ Each right leg up is one rep. Do three times desired reps for this exercise.

# Any Time Exercises

## #19  Lift the Table

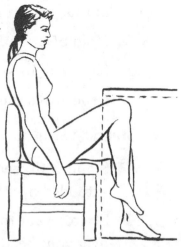

■ Sit at a table, desk, or a restaurant booth.

■ Lift one leg so knee touches underside of table.

■ Press upward as if to lift the table. Keep up the pressure for 10 seconds.

■ Let that knee down and do the same with the other knee.

■ Repeat alternating legs until both have done the exercise three times.

## #20 Extended Leg Desk Lift

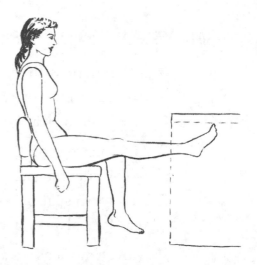

- Push upward with your toe putting pressure on the desk. Hold for 10 seconds.

- Return that foot to the floor.

- Do the same with the other foot holding pressure for 10 seconds.

- Now repeat the exercise until each leg has done the exercise three times.

## #21 Chair Lean Back

- Sit on very front edge of a chair or bench. Arms crossed, feet together on floor. Lean back slowly until your back almost touches the chair. If you don't feel a strain on your stomach muscles, move out farther on the front edge of the chair.

- Hold position for 10 seconds.

- Slowly sit forward.

- Repeat this exercise six times.

## #22 Standing Stretch

- Stand with feet a foot apart, right hand on hip, left arm extended over head.

- Stretch your torso slowly to the right, stretching your left hand over your head to the right. Stretch as far as you can five times.

- Change hands and do the same thing to the left.

- Repeat the left-right exercises three times.

## #23 Lean Back, Lift Knees

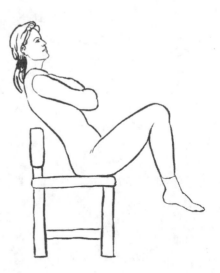

- Sit on very front edge of a chair. Both feet resting on the floor, arms folded on chest.

- Lean back slowly without touching back of the chair. At the same time, lift your knees off the floor. Stress muscles. Hold for a five count.

- Return to start position.

- Repeat 10 times.

## #24 Standing Trunk Turner

- Stand with feet a foot apart, and hands clasped behind head. Elbows pushed to the rear as far as possible.

- Lift your right knee as high as possible directly in front of you.

- At the same time, bend and reach down with your left elbow to touch your right knee.

- Return to start position.

- Do the exercise again with right elbow touching the left knee.

- Repeat three times each direction

# Another Check on Your Eating Habits

There has been a lot of talk about eating in this book. That's good, but we didn't cover the whole subject. Green leafy vegetables, fish, and whole grain cereals are good, and good for us, but how do they compare with some of the more common foods we eat every day and perhaps should start to stay away from.

The list does not show the beta-carotene in each product, but does show the amount of fat and calories in each one. It's an interesting study on its own.

This is one more way to encourage you to eat a "high health for your eyes" diet. These charts should help you to do that.

## Food Chart Showing Fat Grams Per Serving

The following foods are listed in category alphabetically. They are listed by food group, not as "apple" but apple is shown under fruit. Some products are listed by themselves, but all are in categories such as: bread, cakes, eggs, margarine, or pasta.

Since many of us are also interested in the calorie count on food, I'll also list the calories for each serving. Note: T in the fat grams column means "trace."

| Food | Serving | Fat (g) | Cals |
|------|---------|---------|------|
| **BACON** | | | |
| Armour Star, cooked | 1 slice | 3 | 38 |
| Oscar Mayer, cooked | 1 slice | 3 | 35 |
| Nathan's Beef Bacon | 3 slices | 7 | 100 |
| **BEEF** | | | |
| Tenderloin | 3 oz | 12 | 208 |
| Top round | 3 oz | 8 | 170 |
| Top sirloin, fried | 3 oz | 19 | 277 |
| **BEER** | | | |
| Schlitz | 12 oz | 0 | 145 |
| Miller Lite | 12 oz | 0 | 96 |
| **BREAD** | | | |
| Weight Watcher's Cinnamon Raisin | 1 slice | T | 60 |
| Pepperidge Farms | 1 slice | 3 | 90 |
| Wonder, Wheat | 1 slice | 1 | 70 |
| Light Oatmeal | 1 slice | 0 | 45 |
| Pita, whole wheat | 1 oz | 1 | 80 |
| Roman Meal | 1 slice | 1 | 68 |
| French bread | 1 slice | 1 | 100 |
| **BUTTER** | | | |
| Cabot | 1 tsp | 4 | 35 |
| Land O'Lakes | 1 tsp | 4 | 35 |
| Land O'Lakes Whip | 1 tsp | 3 | 25 |
| **CAKE MIXES** | | | |
| Angel food | 1/12 cake | 0 | 150 |
| Banana cake | 1/12 cake | 11 | 250 |
| Carrot cake | 1/12 cake | 15 | 232 |
| Chocolate & Chocolate frosting | 1/8 cake | 17 | 300 |
| Date quick bread | 1/12 loaf | 2 | 160 |
| Lemon cake, frosting | 1/8 cake | 17 | 300 |
| Crumb coffeecake | 1/6 cake | 7 | 230 |

| Food | Serving | Fat (g) | Cals |
|------|---------|---------|------|
| **CANDY** | | | |
| Almond Joy | 1.76 oz | 14 | 250 |
| Butterfinger | 2.1 oz | 12 | 280 |
| Hershey Bar w/Almonds | 1.45 oz | 14 | 240 |
| Lifesavers | 1 candy | 0 | 40 |
| M & M Peanuts | 1.7 oz | 13 | 250 |
| Mr. GoodBar | 1.7 oz | 19 | 290 |
| Gum drops | 1 oz | 0 | 100 |
| **CEREALS (WITH ½ CUP 1% MILK)** | | | |
| Alpha Bits | 1 cup | 1.5 | 212 |
| 100% Bran | 1/3 cup | 3.5 | 170 |
| Apple Raisin Crisp | 2/3 cup | 1.5 | 230 |
| Bran Flakes | 1 oz | 2.5 | 200 |
| Raltson Rice Chex | 1 cup | 1.5 | 194 |
| Froot Loops | 1 cup | 2.5 | 210 |
| Corn Flakes | 1 cup | 1.5 | 210 |
| Quaker Life | 2/3 cup | 3.5 | 200 |
| Quaker 100% Natural | ¼ cup | 7.5 | 227 |
| Cream of Wheat | 1 oz | 2.5 | 208 |
| Instant oatmeal | 1 cup | 3.5 | 245 |
| **CHEESE** | | | |
| Blue cheese | 1 oz | 8 | 100 |
| Brie | 1 oz | 8 | 95 |
| Armour Cheddar | 1 oz | 9 | 110 |
| Bristol Gold Lite | 1 oz | 4 | 70 |
| Colby | 1 oz | 9 | 110 |
| Edam | 1 oz | 8 | 100 |
| Kraft Gouda | 1 oz | 9 | 110 |
| Monterey Jack | 1 oz | 9 | 110 |
| Swiss | 1 oz | 8 | 110 |
| **CHICKEN** | | | |
| Breast quarters w/skin | 1 oz | 2 | 42 |
| Breast quarters skinless | 1 oz | T | 31 |

| Food | Serving | Fat (g) | Cals |
|---|---|---|---|
| Leg quarters w/skin | 1 oz | 4 | 49 |
| Dark meat batter dip | 5.9 oz | 31 | 497 |
| Dark meat, roasted | 3.5 oz | 16 | 256 |
| Banquet Fried Chicken | 6.4 oz | 19 | 330 |
| Swanson Fried Chicken | 4.5 oz | 20 | 360 |
| **CHILI** | | | |
| Chef Boyardee Chili Con Carne w/ Beans | 7 oz | 20 | 340 |
| Dennison's Chili w/ Beans | 7.5 oz | 19 | 300 |
| Van Camp's Chili w/ Beans | 1 cup | 23 | 352 |
| Health Valley Vegetarian | 5 oz | 3 | 160 |
| **POTATO CHIPS** | | | |
| Eagle Chips | 1 oz | 10 | 150 |
| Kelly's Rippled | 1 oz | 9 | 150 |
| Lance Rippled | 1 oz | 13 | 160 |
| Pringle's Chips | 1 oz | 13 | 170 |
| Weight Watchers Barbecue | 1 oz | 6 | 140 |
| **COFFEE** | | | |
| Instant Regular, black | 6 oz | 0 | 4 |
| Regular brewed, black | 6 oz | 0 | 4 |
| **COOKIES, READY TO EAT** | | | |
| Nabisco Raisin Oatmeal | 1 | 3 | 70 |
| Angel Bars | 1 | 5 | 74 |
| Lance Apple Oatmeal | 1.65 oz | 7 | 190 |
| Anisette Toast Jumbo | 1 | 1 | 109 |
| Chips Ahoy Choc-Walnut | 1 | 6 | 100 |
| Nutra/Balance Choc Chip | 2 oz | 14 | 260 |
| Lance Choc-O-Mint | 1.25 oz | 10 | 180 |
| Health Valley Apple Spice | 3 | T | 75 |
| Tastykake Fudge Bar | 1 | 8 | 240 |
| Frookie Ginger Spice | 1 | 2 | 45 |
| Sunshine Lemon Coolers | 2 | 2 | 60 |
| **COTTAGE CHEESE** | | | |
| Borden 5% Dry Curd | ½ cup | 1 | 80 |

| Food | Serving | Fat (g) | Cals |
|------|---------|---------|------|
| Knudsen 2% | 4 oz | 2 | 100 |
| Land O'Lakes | 4 oz | 5 | 120 |
| Weight Watchers 1% | ½ cup | 1 | 90 |
| **CRACKERS** | | | |
| Nabisco Cracked Wheat | 4 | 4 | 70 |
| Goya Butter Crackers | 1 | 1 | 40 |
| Cheese crackers w/Peanut butter | 1.4 oz | 11 | 210 |
| Cheez-it | 12 | 4 | 70 |
| Dark Rye Crisp Bread | 1 | T | 26 |
| Nabisco Escort | 3 | 4 | 70 |
| Keebler Garlic Melba toast | 2 | T | 25 |
| Saltines | 2 | 1 | 25 |
| **FROZEN DINNERS** | | | |
| Armour Classic Chick/Noodles | 11 oz | 73 | 230 |
| Armour Lite Chicken Ala King | 11 oz | 7 | 290 |
| Banquet Chicken Nuggets | 6 | 16 | 340 |
| Budget Gourmet Chicken Caccitori | 1 pkg. | 27 | 470 |
| Budget Gourmet Lite Pot Roast | 1 pkg. | 8 | 210 |
| Le Menu Beef Stroganoff | 10 oz | 4 | 430 |
| Le Menu Lite Glazed Chicken | 10 oz | 3 | 230 |
| Lean Cuisine Fillet Fish | 10 oz | 5 | 210 |
| Swanson Chicken Nuggets | 9 oz | 23 | 470 |
| Weight Watchers Baked Fish | 7 oz | 4 | 150 |
| **DOUGHNUTS** | | | |
| Tastykake Chocolate Dipped | 1 | 10 | 181 |
| Earth Grains Devil's Food | 1 | 21 | 330 |
| Powdered sugar minis | 1 | 3 | 58 |
| Tastykake Fudge Iced | 1 | 21 | 350 |
| Glazed donuts | 1 | 13 | 235 |
| **EGGS** | | | |
| Fried with margarine | 1 | 7 | 91 |
| Hard boiled | 1 | 5 | 77 |
| Scrambled | 1 | 7 | 101 |

| Food | Serving | Fat (g) | Cals |
|---|---|---|---|
| Egg white only | 1 | 0 | 17 |
| One egg yolk poached | 1 | 5 | 59 |
| Egg Beaters (substitute) | ¼ cup | 0 | 25 |
| Scrambled (substitute) | 3.5 oz | 5 | 105 |
| **FISH** | | | |
| Smelt | 6 oz | 6 | 212 |
| Red snapper | 6 oz | 3 | 217 |
| Microwave tuna sandwich | 1 | 6 | 200 |
| Rainbow trout broiled | 3 oz | 4 | 129 |
| Canned tuna in water | 3 oz | 2 | 90 |
| Canned tuna in oil | 3 oz | 15 | 200 |
| S&W canned tuna in water | 3 oz | 1.5 | 90 |
| Orange ruffy baked | 3 oz | 1 | 75 |
| Sea bass, broiled | 3 oz | 2 | 105 |
| Groton's Frozen Scrod | 1 pkg. | 18 | 320 |
| Van Kamp's Frozen Fillets | 1 | 10 | 180 |
| Mrs. Paul's Fish Cakes | 2 | 7 | 190 |
| Microwave Fish Sandwich | 1 | 15 | 280 |
| **FRUIT\*** | | | |
| Fresh apple | 1 | T | 81 |
| Fresh grapefruit | ½ | 0 | 40 |
| Dry, pitted prunes | ¼ cup | 1 | 140 |
| Fresh orange | 1 | T | 69 |
| Fresh pear | 1 | 1 | 100 |
| Fresh pineapple | 1 cup | 1 | 90 |
| Canned mixed fruit | ½ cup | 0 | 90 |
| **FRENCH TOAST** | | | |
| Home-made with egg, milk | 1 slice | 7 | 155 |
| Take-out, with butter | 1 slice | 9 | 180 |
| Aunt Jemima Cinnamon Swirls | 3 oz | 4 | 71 |
| Weight Watchers French Toast | 2 slices | 5 | 160 |
| **GELATIN** | | | |
| Royal Apple | ½ cup | 0 | 80 |

\* Most fresh fruits have almost no grams of fat. Canned fruits have little more, but the sugar content raises the calorie count.

| Food | Serving | Fat (g) | Cals |
|------|---------|---------|------|
| Jell-O Black Raspberry | ½ cup | T | 81 |
| Cherry w/Nutrasweet | ½ cup | T | 8 |
| Diamond Crystal Orange, sugar-free | ½ cup | T | 9 |
| **GRAVY (CANNED)** | | | |
| Franco-American Beef | 2 oz | 1 | 25 |
| Franco-American Pork | 2 oz | 3 | 40 |
| Pepperidge Farm Beef | 2 oz | 2.5 | 65 |
| **HAM** | | | |
| Armour Star Boneless | 1 oz | 2 | 41 |
| Hansel'n Gretel Deluxe | 1 oz | 1 | 31 |
| Krakus Polish cooked | 1 oz | 3 | 65 |
| Oscar Mayer Cracked Black | 1 oz | T | 24 |
| Russer Lill' Salt cooked | 1 oz | 1 | 30 |
| Canned extra lean | 1 oz | 2 | 41 |
| **HAMBURGER** | | | |
| Double patty w/bun | 1 reg. | 28 | 544 |
| Double patty, all fixings | 1 reg. | 32 | 576 |
| Double patty, all fixings | 1 large | 44 | 706 |
| Single patty w/bun | 1 reg. | 12 | 275 |
| Single patty, bun, cheese | 1 reg. | 15 | 320 |
| Single patty, all fixings | 1 large | 48 | 745 |
| Triple patty, all fixings | 1 large | 51 | 769 |
| **HOT DOGS** | | | |
| *Chicken:* | | | |
| Health Valley | 1 | 8 | 96 |
| Weaver | 1 | 10 | 115 |
| *Turkey:* | | | |
| Bil Mar Cheese Franks | 1 | 9 | 109 |
| Louis Rich | 1 | 9 | 103 |
| Mr. Turkey Franks | 1 | 11 | 132 |
| Wampler Longacre | 1 | 31 | 102 |
| *Beef:* | | | |

| Food | Serving | Fat (g) | Cals |
|---|---|---|---|
| Armour Star Jumbo | 1 | 18 | 170 |
| Hebrew National | 1 | 15 | 160 |
| Oscar Mayer Bun Lengths | 1 | 17 | 186 |
| Oscar Mayer Wieners Little | 1 | 3 | 28 |
| **ICE CREAM, ICE DESERTS** | | | |
| Bresler's All Flavors Ice | 3.5 oz | 0 | 120 |
| Bresler's Ice Cream | 3.5 oz | 12 | 230 |
| Edy's light Almond Praline | 4 oz | 5 | 140 |
| Sealtest Butter Crunch | ½ cup | 9 | 160 |
| Lady Borden Butter Pecan | ½ cup | 12 | 180 |
| Haagen-Daz Chocolate | 4 oz | 17 | 270 |
| Weight Watchers Ice Milk | ½ cup | 4 | 120 |
| Ben & Jerry's Chocolate Fudge | 4 oz | 16 | 280 |
| Good Humor Chocolate Malt | 3 oz | 13 | 187 |
| Weight Watchers Treat Bar | 2.75 oz | 0 | 90 |
| Breyers Coffee Ice Cream | ½ cup | 8 | 150 |
| Mocha Mix Dutch Chocolate | 3.5 oz | 12 | 210 |
| Land O'Lakes Fruit Sherbet | 4 oz | 2 | 130 |
| Wyler's Fruit Punch Slush | 4 oz | 0 | 140 |
| Ben & Jerry's Health Bar | 4 oz | 17 | 300 |
| Jell-O Orange Bars | 1 | T | 42 |
| Borden Orange Sherbet | ½ cup | 1 | 110 |
| **JAMS, JELLIES*** | | | |
| Smucker's Fruit Spreads | 1 tsp | 0 | 16 |
| Pritkin Fruit Spreads | 1 tsp | 0 | 14 |
| White House Apple Butter | 1 oz | 0 | 50 |
| Bama Grape Jelly | 2 tsp | 0 | 25 |
| Apple Jelly | 3.5 oz | 0 | 259 |
| Strawberry Jam | 3.5 oz | 0 | 234 |
| Plum Jam | 3.5 oz | 0 | 241 |
| **LUNCHEON COLD CUTS** | | | |
| Armour Bologna Beef | 1 oz | 8 | 90 |
| Carl Buddig Pastrami | 1 oz | 2 | 40 |
| Hansel'N Gretel Healthy Deli | 1 oz | 2 | 41 |

* No jams, jellies, fruit preserves, etc. have any fat grams. The only difference is in the calorie content.

| Food | Serving | Fat (g) | Cals |
|---|---|---|---|
| **BOLOGNA BEEF & PORK** | | | |
| Oscar Mayer Bologna | 1 slice | 8 | 90 |
| Oscar Mayer Honey Loaf | 1 slice | 1 | 35 |
| Weight Watchers Bologna | 1 slice | 1 | 18 |
| Hard Pork Salami | 1 slice | 4 | 41 |
| Summer Sausage Thuringer | 1 oz | 8 | 98 |
| **MARGARINE** | | | |
| Fleischmann's Diet | 1 tbsp | 6 | 50 |
| Mazola Diet | 1 tbsp | 6 | 50 |
| Parkay Diet Soft | 1 tbsp | 6 | 50 |
| Smart Beat | 1 tbsp | 3 | 25 |
| *Regular Stick:* | | | |
| Blue Bonnet | 1 tbsp | 11 | 100 |
| Fleischmann's | 1 tbsp | 11 | 100 |
| Land O'Lakes | 1 tbsp | 4 | 35 |
| Mazola | 1 tbsp | 11 | 100 |
| Parkay | 1 tbsp | 11 | 100 |
| *Soft Tub:* | | | |
| Blue Bonnet | 1 tbsp | 11 | 100 |
| Fleischmann's | 1 tbsp | 11 | 100 |
| Land O'Lakes Tub | 1 tbsp | 4 | 35 |
| Parkway Soft | 1 tbsp | 11 | 100 |
| Promise | 1 tbsp | 10 | 90 |
| Parkay Whipped | 1 tbsp | 7 | 70 |
| **MAYONNAISE** | | | |
| *Low Calorie:* | | | |
| Best Foods Cholesterol Free | 1 tbsp | 5 | 50 |
| Best Foods Light | 1 tbsp | 5 | 50 |
| Kraft Free | 1 tbsp | 0 | 12 |
| Kraft Light | 1 tbsp | 5 | 50 |
| Smart Beat Corn Oil | 1 tbsp | 4 | 40 |
| *Regular:* | | | |
| Best Foods Real | 1 tbsp | 11 | 100 |
| Hellmann's Real | 1 tbsp | 11 | 100 |

| Food | Serving | Fat (g) | Cals |
|---|---|---|---|
| Kraft Real | 1 tbsp | 12 | 100 |
| Sandwich Spread | 1 tbsp | 5 | 60 |
| **MEXICAN FOOD FROZEN** | | | |
| Banquet Chimichanga | 9.5 oz | 21 | 480 |
| Banquet Enchilada Cheese | 11 oz | 9 | 340 |
| El Charrito Burrito Grande | 6 oz | 16 | 430 |
| Enchilada Cheese Dinner | 14 oz | 24 | 570 |
| Corn tortillas | 2 | 1 | 95 |
| Healthy choice Enchiladas | 13 oz | 5 | 350 |
| Healthy Choice Fajitas | 7 oz | 4 | 210 |
| Lean Cuisine Enchanadas | 10 oz | 9 | 290 |
| Patio Enchilada Beef Dinner | 13 oz | 24 | 520 |
| Patio Fiesta Dinner | 12 oz | 20 | 460 |
| Van De Kamp's Beef Burrito | 5 | 9 | 320 |
| Van De Kamp's Mexican Classics: | | | |
| Chicken Suiza w/ Rice, Beans | 15 oz | 20 | 550 |
| Enchilada Suiza Chicken | 5.5 oz | 10 | 220 |
| Weight Watchers Fajitas | 7 oz | 5 | 210 |
| Taco shells | 1 | 2 | 50 |
| **MUFFINS** | | | |
| *Frozen:* | | | |
| Sara Lee Apple Oat Bran | 1 | 6 | 190 |
| Health Valley Banana Free | 1 | T | 130 |
| Sara Lee Blueberry | 1 | 8 | 200 |
| Sara Lee Blueberry Free | 1 | 0 | 120 |
| Peppridge Farm Cinnamon Swirl | 1 | 6 | 190 |
| Sara Lee Golden Corn | 1 | 13 | 240 |
| Health Valley Oat Bran | 1 | 4 | 140 |
| *Muffin Box Mix:* | | | |
| Arrowhead Blue Corn | 1 | 4 | 110 |
| Duncan Hines Bran, Honey | 1 | 4 | 120 |
| Duncan Hines Cran-nut | 1 | 8 | 200 |
| Duncan Hines Wild Blueberry | 1 | 3 | 110 |

| Food | Serving | Fat (g) | Cals |
|------|---------|---------|------|
| **MILK** | | | |
| Evaporated | ½ cup | 10 | 170 |
| Evaporated Skim | ½ cup | 0 | 100 |
| Carnation dry milk | 8 oz | T | 90 |
| 1% Milk | ½ cup | 1.5 | 51 |
| 2% milk | ½ cup | 2.5 | 60 |
| Buttermilk | ½ cup | 2 | 60 |
| Whole milk regular | ½ cup | 4 | 75 |
| Skim milk | ½ cup | T | 45 |
| **NUTS** | | | |
| Cashews, peanuts | 1 oz | 12 | 170 |
| Planters Mixed, Salted | 1 oz | 15 | 170 |
| Guy's Tasty Mix | 1 oz | 7 | 130 |
| Dry roasted w/peanuts | 1 oz | 15 | 169 |
| Planters' Almonds | 1 oz | 15 | 170 |
| Black Walnuts | 1 oz | 17 | 180 |
| English Walnut Halves | 1 oz | 20 | 190 |
| Cashews | 1 oz | 14 | 170 |
| Cashews dry roasted | 1 oz | 13 | 163 |
| Filberts | 1 oz | 19 | 191 |
| Peanuts dry roasted | 1 oz | 14 | 170 |
| Peanut butter | 2 tbsp | 17 | 200 |
| Pecans | 1 oz | 20 | 190 |
| **OIL, COOKING** | | | |
| Crisco | 1 tbsp | 14 | 120 |
| Planter's Popcorn Oil | 1 tbsp | 13 | 120 |
| Puritan | 1 tbsp | 14 | 120 |
| Wesson Corn | 1 tbsp | 14 | 120 |
| Smart Beat | 1 tbsp | 14 | 120 |
| Wesson Vegetable | 1 tbsp | 14 | 120 |
| Crisco Solid | 1 tbsp | 12 | 110 |
| Wesson Shortening | 1 tbsp | 12 | 100 |
| **ORIENTAL FOODS (FROZEN)** | | | |

| Food | Serving | Fat (g) | Cals |
|---|---|---|---|
| Benihana Lites Chicken | 9 oz | 4 | 270 |
| Birds Eye Stir Fry Vegetables | ½ cup | T | 36 |
| Birds Eye Chow Mein | ½ cup | 4 | 89 |
| Chung King Walnut Chicken | 13 oz | 5 | 310 |
| Chung King Egg Rolls Shrimp | 3.6 oz | 6 | 200 |
| La Choy Pork Egg Roll | 3 oz | 5 | 150 |
| *Take Out:* | | | |
| Chicken teriyaki | ¾ oz | 27 | 399 |
| Chop suey with pork | 1 cup | 24 | 425 |
| **PANCAKES AND WAFFLES** | | | |
| *From Mixes Made At Home:* | | | |
| Hungry Jack Blueberry | 3 4-inch | 15 | 320 |
| Aunt Jemima Buckwheat | 3 4-inch | 8 | 230 |
| Hungry Jack Buttermilk | 3 4-inch | 11 | 240 |
| Hungry Jack Packets | 3 4-inch | 3 | 180 |
| Arrowhead Griddle Lite | ½ cup | 3 | 260 |
| Estee Pancake Mix | 3 3-inch | 0 | 100 |
| Pancakes with butter, syrup | 3 4-inch | 14 | 519 |
| **PASTA*** | | | |
| Dry pasta, all types | 2 oz | 1 | 210 |
| *Pasta dinners, frozen:* | | | |
| Banquet entree Primavera | 7 oz | 3 | 140 |
| Banquet Macaroni & Cheese | 7 oz | 11 | 260 |
| Budget Gourmet Stroganoff | 1 pkg | 12 | 290 |
| Budget Gourmet Cheese Manicotti | 1 pkg | 25 | 430 |
| Dining Light Fettuccini | 1 pkg | 9 | 260 |
| Healthy Choice Fettuccini | 8.5 oz | 4 | 240 |
| Kid Cuisine Macaroni, Franks | 9 oz | 15 | 360 |
| Le Menu Light Tortellini | 8 oz | 8 | 250 |
| Lean Cuisine Rigatoni, Meat | 10 oz | 10 | 260 |
| Morton Macaroni & Cheese | 6.5 oz | 14 | 290 |
| Swanson Spaghetti and Meat Balls | 13 oz | 18 | 490 |
| Weight Watchers Manicotti | 10 oz | 8 | 260 |

* Most pastas are 1 gram of fat per 2 oz. The differential here is what is put in the pasta or on it. Calories for plain pasta range from 160 per 2 oz to 210.

| Food | Serving | Fat (g) | Cals |
|---|---|---|---|
| **PIE** | | | |
| *Frozen:* | | | |
| Banquet Apple | | | |
| Sara Lee Apple | 1 slice | 11 | 250 |
| Mrs. Smith's Apple Natural | 1 slice | 12 | 280 |
| Banquet Banana | 1 slice | 22 | 420 |
| Mrs. Smith's Blueberry | 1 slice | 10 | 180 |
| Banquet Lemon | 1 slice | 17 | 380 |
| Banquet Pumpkin | 1 slice | 9 | 170 |
| *Baked Ready to Eat:* | 1 slice | 8 | 200 |
| Apple | | | |
| Creme | | | |
| Lemon meringue | 1 slice | 18 | 405 |
| | 1 slice | 23 | 455 |
| **PIZZA, FROZEN** | 1 slice | 14 | 355 |
| Celeste Deluxe | | | |
| Fox Deluxe Sausage | | | |
| Jeno's 4 Pack Cheese | 8 oz | 32 | 600 |
| Jeno's Crisp Sausage | ½ pizza | 13 | 260 |
| Pappalo's French Pepperoni | 1 pizza | 8 | 160 |
| Totino's Bacon Party | ½ pizza | 16 | 300 |
| Totino's Mexican Style | 1 pizza | 20 | 410 |
| Weight Watcher's Cheese | ½ pizza | 20 | 370 |
| | ½ pizza | 21 | 380 |
| **POPCORN** | 7 oz | 7 | 300 |
| Jiffy Pop Microwave Butter | | | |
| Newman's Microwave Light | | | |
| Redenbacher Gourmet Original | 4 cups | 7 | 140 |
| Pillsbury Microwave Butter | 3 cups | 3 | 90 |
| Ultra Slim-Fast Lite | 3 cups | 4 | 80 |
| Weight Watcher's Ready Eat | 3 cups | 13 | 210 |
| | ½ oz | 2 | 60 |
| **SALAD DRESSING** | .7 oz | 3 | 90 |
| *Ready To Use:* | | | |
| Catalina | | | |
| Diamond Crystal Blue Cheese | | | |

| Food | Serving | Fat (g) | Cals |
|---|---|---|---|
| Kraft Bacon & Tomato | 1 tbsp | 1 | 15 |
| Kraft Free Catalina Nonfat | 1 tbsp | 1 | 20 |
| Ott's Italian Chef | 1 tbsp | 7 | 70 |
| Newman's Olive Oil and Vinegar | 1 tbsp | 0 | 20 |
| Seven Seas Free Ranch Nonfat | 1 tbsp | 9 | 80 |
| *Ready To Use Lite:* | 1 tbsp | 9 | 80 |
| Estee Blue Cheese | 1 tbsp | 0 | 16 |
| Herb Magic Vinaigrette | | | |
| Kraft French | 1 tbsp | T | 8 |
| Magic Mountain Blue Cheese | 1 tbsp | 0 | 6 |
| S&W Italian No Oil | 1 tbsp | 1 | 20 |
| Ultra Slim-Fast | 1 tbsp | T | 5 |
| Weight Watcher's Russian | 1 tbsp | 0 | 2 |
| | 1 tbsp | T | 6 |
| **SAUSAGE** | 1 tbsp | 5 | 50 |
| Oscar Mayer Bratwurst, Smoked | | | |
| Perdue Turkey Patties | | | |
| Armour Country Sausage | 2.7 oz | 21 | 237 |
| Hebrew National Knockwurst | 1.3 oz | 4 | 61 |
| Oscar Mayer Polish | 1 oz | 11 | 110 |
| Armour Link Pork Sausage | 3 oz | 25 | 260 |
| Perdue Sweet Italian Turkey | 2.7 oz | 20 | 229 |
| **SODA DRINKS*** | 1 oz | 11 | 110 |
| | 2 oz | 6 | 94 |
| **SOUP** | | | |
| *Canned:* | | | |
| Healthy Choice Bean & Ham | | | |
| Campbell Bean w/bacon | | | |
| College Inn Beef Broth | 7.5 oz | 4 | 220 |
| Campbell Beef Noodle | 8 oz | 4 | 140 |
| Lipton Beef Noodle | 7 oz | 0 | 16 |
| Goya Black Bean | 8 oz | 3 | 70 |
| Gold's Borscht | 8 oz | T | 85 |
| Health Valley Chicken Broth | 7.5 oz | 4 | 160 |

* All but four of the popular soft drinks now on the market have no fat grams at all. Of the four that do, two are root beer, one a ginger ale and the other a wild berry. Calories vary but go from a low of a trace in diet drinks to 190. Most are about 75 or 80 calories. No big worry about fat grams from soft drinks.

| Food | Serving | Fat (g) | Cals |
|------|---------|---------|------|
| Campbell Chicken Corn Chowder | 8 oz | 0 | 100 |
| Pritikin Lentil | 7.5 oz | 2 | 35 |
| Snow's Clam Chowder | 11 oz | 21 | 340 |
| Health Valley Minestrone | 7 oz | 0 | 100 |
| American New England Chowder | 7.5 oz | 2 | 70 |
| Pritikin Split Pea | 7.5 oz | 3 | 130 |
| Campbell Tomato 2% milk | 4 oz | 6 | 145 |
| Campbell Vegetable | 7.5 oz | T | 130 |
| | 8 oz | 2 | 90 |
| **TURKEY** | 8 oz | 2 | 90 |
| *Fresh:* | | | |
| Louis Rich Breast | | | |
| Perdue Breast Fillets | | | |
| Louis Rich Breast Steaks | 1 oz | 2 | 50 |
| Perdue Fresh Drumsticks | 1 oz | T | 28 |
| Bill Mar Ground Turkey | 1 oz | T | 40 |
| Louis Rich Thighs | 1 oz | 2 | 36 |
| Shady Brook Wings | 3 oz | 12 | 163 |
| Whole Turkey | 1 oz | 4 | 65 |
| | 3 oz | 6 | 130 |
| **VEGETABLES** | 3.5 oz | 10 | 200 |
| Hanover broccoli, cauliflower | | | |
| Broccoli, cauliflower, carrots with cheese sauce | | | |
| Chinese stir fry | ½ cup | 0 | 20 |
| Japanese stir fry | ½ cup | 6 | 89 |
| Mixed vegetables w/onion | ½ cup | T | 36 |
| Oriental blend | ½ cup | T | 29 |
| Peas, onions, cheese sauce | ½ cup | 5 | 97 |
| Stew vegetables | ½ cup | 0 | 25 |
| Peas & onions cooked | ½ cup | 6 | 126 |
| Fresh zucchini | 3 oz | T | 50 |
| Canned tomatoes | ½ cup | T | 40 |
| Canned spinach | ½ oz | T | 3 |
| Fresh shallots, chopped | ½ cup | T | 40 |
| Sauerkraut, canned | ½ cup | 0 | 25 |

| Food | Serving | Fat (g) | Cals |
|------|---------|---------|------|
| Fresh baked potato | 1 tbsp | T | 7 |
| Canned peas | ½ cup | 0 | 20 |
| Canned corn | 5 oz | T | 220 |
| Canned carrots | ½ cup | 0 | 90 |
| | ½ cup | 0 | 70 |
| **YOGURT** | ½ cup | 0 | 20 |
| Cabot all flavors | | | |
| Apples'N Spice No-fat | | | |
| Black Cherry Classic | 8 oz | 3 | 220 |
| Colombo Blueberry Classic | 8 oz | T | 190 |
| Dannon Blueberry No-fat | 8 oz | 6 | 230 |
| Yoplait Blueberry Original | 8 oz | 6 | 230 |
| Knudsen Lemon w/Aspartame | 8 oz | 0 | 100 |
| La Yogurt Peach | 6 oz | 3 | 190 |
| Mountain High Plain | 8 oz | 0 | 70 |
| Meadow Gold Raspberry Sundae | 6 oz | 4 | 190 |
| New Country Strawberry | 8 oz | 9 | 200 |
| | 8 oz | 4 | 250 |
| | 6 oz | 2 | 150 |

# INDEX